NAVIGATING PHD

THINGS TO KNOW BEFORE, DURING AND AFTER PHD

PROF. VIJAYAVENKATARAMAN SANJAIRAJ | PHD

Made with ♥ on the Notion Press Platform
www.notionpress.com

To God Almighty, my all in all

To my mom, who dedicated her life to bringing me up

To my wife, who is my best friend and companion

Contents

Preface

I have been wanting to write a book for a long time! Of course, as a Professor, I do write research articles, book chapters and hopefully books. But I was interested in reaching out to a wider community, writing about my experience in academia and in the process, answering the many questions that people might have. Where do I start?

I had many students ask me about the PhD, if it is worth pursuing, how to select a university, what to look for in a research group, career path in academia or industry and surviving the PhD ordeal! Since I had answered hundreds of them already, I thought that's the first topic that I would want to write about. It might seem very obvious to some while others might find it extremely useful but I would pen down in each of the chapters what my thoughts are, from my experience in interacting with a lot of students, ranging from aspiring undergraduate students, both successful and struggling PhD students, and most-importantly the highly ambiguous **PhinisheD** ones!

The chapters in this book not only just focuses on a set of objective things to look for when you decide on your graduate studies but also is filled with lot of practical things to consider, which I personally felt nobody told me about! Had I known these things before I decided on my graduate studies, I would have been more careful!

I hope the contents of this book would be useful, in one way or the other to you – at least serve as an example of how not to write a book!

I hope I will earn the privilege of your time!
Prof. Vijayavenkataraman Sanjairaj

CHAPTER I

Is a PhD worth pursuing?

I believe everything and everyone in this world has 'inherent' value. Going by my belief, a PhD is definitely worth doing! The question here is whether the 'inherent' value of a PhD is 'intrinsic' or 'instrumental'. I will explain. 'Intrinsic' value is having a value on its own, an 'end-in-itself' while 'instrumental' value depends on its relation with another entity having intrinsic value. These terms are associated with moral philosophy, coined by the sociologist Max Weber. I don't digress, where else to talk about these terms if we don't talk about them to a person interested in gaining a 'Doctor of Philosophy' title?!

Jargons apart, an individual's perception as to whether a PhD is worth pursuing depends on the perspective that one holds regarding the nature of the value of PhD. I want the readers to think a little deeper on these lines to introspect themselves so that they get to understand their own perspectives better. Many were, are, and will be disappointed during or after completing their PhDs because they 'misjudged' the nature of the value of the PhD. Some think PhD has 'intrinsic' value while others think it only carries 'instrumental' values. Many who couldn't cope with it and many others who completed but couldn't attain the level they thought they would achieve on completing their PhD think 'PhD' has no value at all! I would refer you back to the first line of this article to refute this claim.

Before we move on to analyze the nature of the value of a PhD, let us first understand with examples what 'intrinsic' and 'instrumental' values mean. A man possesses a hammer. The value that the hammer carries is to help 'pounding a nail'. In other words, it is an instrument (carrying an instrumental value) used to achieve a specific end (and not an end in itself). Another man possesses 'joy' and 'happiness', which carry intrinsic values. Possessing joy and happiness are 'end-in-itself' (for most humans). At least, for common men, asking 'Why do you want to be joyful?' will seem a stupid question. A hammer is an instrument but 'joy' is an end-in-itself!

Now, we will apply this phenomenon to doing a PhD and discuss a few points why people have different opinions on doing a PhD, and the best way, in my opinion, to approach a PhD. Let us start with the instrumental values of PhD. By now, many would have thought or at least started thinking that PhD is after all a degree, it is an instrument, why would it carry any intrinsic value? I will first give the merits of classifying PhD as having instrumental value. What would doing a PhD give? All the benefits that a PhD is expected to give can be grouped into two: 'Societal approval' and 'financial growth'. First, you will be part of an 'elite' group (less than 2% of the world's population has a PhD!) – 'societal approval'. Second, you might (yes, 'might' not 'will') get a better job, with a better pay – 'financial growth(?)'. You might argue that people do PhD to gain knowledge and skills. If you ask why gain knowledge and skills, it will again lead to 'societal approval' and 'financial growth'.

Many start their PhD search with this perspective of PhD having an instrumental value, pure instrumental value. And, here lies the 'folly'. Sometime during the process or after completing the PhD, when the 'instrument' they carry fails them, they are deeply disappointed. I will explain with examples. First, the thought that PhD would lead to societal approval is broken both during the PhD and after completion. During the PhD, the disappointment (loss of self-esteem) comes in two ways:

1. Interactions with the professors, scientists, researchers or even fellow PhD students 'might' (most of the cases 'will') lead to 'inferiority complex', you will start to believe that you are 'not up to the mark'!
2. You, in your opinion, would have done a wonderful job (an experiment, a manuscript, or a piece of art). When you discuss it with your peers or your supervisor, they might not approve of it (either they are being honest or they couldn't appreciate the depth of your work). What better example can be given than a manuscript being continuously rejected by a number of journals.

Many drop-out of PhD, mainly due to one of the reasons above. After completing your PhD, when you don't get a job, the rest of the 'societal approval' value is shattered as well! You get a feeling that the PhD is not worth it at all, you cannot convince even a single employer of the worth of your PhD!

Second, the financial aspects of doing a PhD. While it is a common knowledge (at least to the people in academia) that the stipend people get while doing a PhD and the salary they get as a postdoctoral associate or a faculty is relatively lesser than their industrial equivalents (similar pre-doctoral qualification, experience, and skills), people still want to think that PhD will pay them dividends for all the hard-work! But, when they face the reality of landing in a post-doctoral position or a faculty position with a pay much lesser than they expected, they begin feeling that a PhD isn't worth anything!

The whole article might sound like ranting or being pessimistic, but I am talking about the perspectives here. I am an example myself where PhD has given me both, the 'societal approval' and 'financial growth'. It is important to define or refine your expectations before you decide to take up a PhD. My advice to all who are thinking of a PhD is to set your expectations based on a 'balanced' valuation of the 'intrinsic' and 'instrumental' components! Don't set your expectations purely on the 'instrumental' values of PhD in getting a name for yourself or growing your wealth (these are important and we will talk about them in detail in the later chapters). Give importance also to the 'intrinsic' value of a PhD, the joy of doing a PhD, learning something new, doing something better than what has already been done or what hasn't been done yet, adding value to the society we live in through arts, science, humanities or engineering advancements and deriving happiness purely out of the experience of doing a PhD! Consider PhD to be an 'end-in-itself' phenomenon! By doing so, anything that comes along, be it a publication in your dream journal, a patent or a start-up, a post-doctoral or faculty position in a top university or a university of your choice, or any job or promotion with a decent salary or a hefty pay, regardless of the quantum, will bring joy!

So, is a PhD worth pursuing? Of course, YES!

But, is it for all? Of course, NO!

We will talk about the flip-side of doing a PhD, who consider PhD only for the 'instrumental' values it carries, which are important to survive in this world!

" *My advice to all who are thinking of a PhD is to set your expectations based on a 'balanced' valuation of the 'intrinsic' and 'instrumental'* values! Don't set your expectations purely on the 'instrumental' values of PhD in getting a name for yourself or growing your wealth but give importance also to the 'intrinsic' value of a PhD, the joy of doing a PhD, learning something new, doing something better than what has already been done or what hasn't been done yet, adding value to the society we live in through arts, science, humanities or engineering advancements and deriving happiness purely out of the experience of doing a PhD!

– Vijayavenkataraman Sanjairaj"

"*Consider PhD to be an 'end-in-itself' phenomenon! By doing so, anything that comes along, be it a publication in your dream journal, a patent or a start-up, a post-doctoral or faculty position in a top university or a university of your choice, or any job or promotion with a decent salary or a hefty pay, regardless of the quantum, will bring joy!*

– Vijayavenkataraman Sanjairaj"

CHAPTER II

The flip side of doing a PhD?

We talked about the intrinsic and instrumental value of PhD and the importance of giving equal importance to the intrinsic value as much as the instrumental value. But, the significance of the instrumental value, be it the stipend and time commitment during the PhD and the future prospects after doing a PhD, cannot be underestimated. We will see the flip side of doing a PhD in this article.

Climbing down the career ladder

Yes, you read that right! Given the fact that there are too few academic jobs, most PhD graduates stagnate in one of many post-doctoral positions or research associates (glorified post-docs with a higher pay). People who are frustrated with such positions look out for positions in the industry. When they do so, to their shock and dismay, they find they had actually *climbed down the career ladder*! I foresee two classes of people and I had experienced being in one of the two classes.

The first class of people are those who went on a continuous educational spree, from high school to college / university, undergraduate, master's and PhD. If you belong to this class or are planning to become one, then this is for you. Take the example of Gary. Gary finished his undergraduate degree with flying colors and got admitted into a graduate (Master's) program of a prestigious university. To his disappointment, his best buddy Rachel joined a company as a trainee. When Gary finished his

Master's after 2 years, he was fresh into the job market while Rachel already had acquired 2 years of industrial experience. Although Gary had acquired advanced knowledge and skills from his Master's program, many companies preferred Rachel as she had hands-on experience. Now, one might argue that the starting pay would be higher for Gary (which might be true depending on the field), Rachel has a chance to catch up with accumulating years of experience. While the differences in pay or job opportunities might not be significant between the undergraduate and master's degrees, it plays a huge role when it comes to PhD because getting a PhD takes anywhere between 3 to 5 years on average (depending on various factors including the country of study). A period of 5 years is a significantly higher amount of time in the industry and most people are promoted to the next level. Assume Gary had gone for a PhD and took 4 more years to complete. Rachel will have 6 years of industrial experience while Gary would be a fresher in the job market. Like it or not, industries are not matured enough to consider your PhD years into the years of experience count. They still see 'PhD' as a degree and not as an 'experience'!

The second class of people are those who had disjointed industrial experience during the course of their education. To this class, I belong. Right after my undergraduate education, I went on to work in a manufacturing industry for 3 years before I took up a PhD position. I was clear in my objective of doing a PhD right from the beginning that I want to become a professor! In fact, I left the company to join a PhD to achieve my goal / dream of becoming a professor. I will talk about my whole experience of this transition later in one of the articles. The point I am leading to is, although I was clear of my goal, during the final year of my PhD, I wanted to do a social experiment on finding the place of PhDs in the job market. I decided to go to the annual career fair that happens in my university and talk to the recruiters (not to submit my CV but to talk). Though I was not keen on getting a job and in fact I already had a postdoc offer at hand, I was infuriated after talking to representatives from 5 companies. I had an undergraduate degree from a prestigious institution in India, worked for 3 years in a reputed American company, and did my PhD in a world-renowned institution in Singapore and you know what they said? I just finished my degree and they would only consider me as a fresher!! I asked them if the 3 years of experience that I had before doing my PhD counted, they said no! I still don't understand the logic behind it! I talked to 5 companies and all of them had the same standard response! And I asked them another question about the pay. Will I be paid higher than the undergraduate or Master's degree graduates because I have a PhD? The answer was again negative, some companies buttered saying that the pay 'might' be raised after the initial training period but the bare truth is, I will only be considered as a fresher! Some of my friends had to take up the job because they had no other option. I had a friend from my undergraduate university who had acquired 7 years of industrial experience and was employed at Singapore who earned twice the salary offered by these companies to a PhD fresher! I had no regrets of doing a PhD although my PhD stipend was half that of my friend's salary as I was happy about the 'intrinsic' experience of doing a PhD and the perks that come along (I will talk about the perks in a separate article). But I was infuriated because it was unfair!!

Be careful and do consider this scenario before taking up a PhD! If you are fully aware of this fact that you might actually be climbing down your career ladder even before you decide to take up a PhD, you will be in a much better position later because even if things go wrong, you have already prepared your mind! If you are working for a company and take a sabbatical to do a PhD, the scenario is completely different. Also, if you do a PhD much later in life after you earned a respectable position in a company, the scenario is different again. The field also plays a role, a PhD in Management makes more sense than a PhD in Engineering for a senior professional (who doesn't need a PhD anymore but if he is insistent and interested). We will talk more about some of these cases in Chapter 4 on 'Is PhD for me? Personalizing PhD'.

You are overqualified!

Having a PhD will make you overqualified for most of the jobs out there. There are many reasons why you are (or will be) overqualified. The first and foremost reason is that the skill requirement for the majority of the jobs doesn't need specialized advanced skills that a PhD graduate possesses. Even if you are interested in taking up the position, they will not be ready to pay you higher. And even worst, if you are ready to take up the job for the reduced pay, they still might not be interested in you because:

- some may genuinely think 'underpaying is unfair'
- they might fear you wouldn't do 'things' that are normally expected of the job as you might feel it is below your standards

- they might be concerned that you will lose interest in your job soon and retaining you might be a problem; recruiting takes time and companies will always look for 'loyal' (read "long-term") employees
- the 'ego' problems of any industry where you as a PhD holder will be much younger for a managerial position consisting of much 'older' / 'experienced' employees working for you or people in the managerial positions might see a 'competitor' in you

There are definitely exceptions to it and we are only talking about the majority here. One example of an exception that I could think of is nuclear engineering or space technologies, where gaining a Master's or PhD might be much more valuable. One of the many reasons is that the field is very specialized and an undergraduate degree might not even qualify them for a job in the field.

Uncertain time commitments!

Although time duration (or in other words 'scholarship duration') for PhD is fixed in most countries, there are many uncertainties. You might not finish your PhD! I know people whose supervisors didn't allow them to submit their thesis as they didn't meet the 'standards' even after their scholarship duration was over and they refused (or didn't have funds) to pay stipends. Imagine spending 4 years for a PhD with a reduced stipend and not getting a degree. Though these are rare case scenarios, it is not something that doesn't happen! Your PhD might drag longer than you thought! Some supervisors might be willing to pay you but it might take much longer than you expected. Given the challenges in getting a postdoc / faculty position and limited industrial job opportunities, the whole career outlook might become uncertain.

None of these matters if you did an excellent and extraordinary PhD and you are satisfied with the compensation you get in academia or research institutes or if your PhD has such high industrial relevance that will place you in a senior position in the industry. Finishing a PhD on a very high note very successfully depends on too many factors and too few accomplish that feat!

I will talk about personalizing the PhD based on the family commitments, financial situation, personality traits and personal expectations in the next but one chapter, after talking about the perks of doing a PhD in the next one!

CHAPTER III

The perks of doing a PhD

The previous chapter was about the flip side of doing a PhD. I could imagine many of them who 'PhinisheD' and trying to navigate the job market might nod their heads in approval. Well, a PhD is not just about assignments, surveys, experiments, and publications. It is much more than those, it is an experience!

> *"Well, a PhD is not just about assignments, surveys, experiments, and publications. It is much more than that, it is an experience!*
>
> *- Vijayavenkataraman Sanjairaj"*

Keeps you young!

Many of you wonder why? How does a PhD keep one young? Think of a 3- or 4-year-old kid. It will keep asking questions to the extent parents get frustrated! Why is the Sun so big? Why does a cat meow? Why is there no moon today? What is there beyond the sky? 'Inquisitiveness' defines childhood. PhD, done in its true sense, is all about being inquisitive! If you carefully observe the communication between the doctoral students or researchers or Professors, some of the most commonly used words and phrases would be 'interesting' 'Why?' 'How? 'Did you try....?' 'Can we do....? 'I observed', etc. These are all inquisitive words, phrases, and questions.

I sometimes feel the lack of inquisitiveness is what makes a PhD boring and leaves the PhD student frustrated! I can think of two scenarios. One, the widely prevalent system in the academia of 'publish or perish' kills this inquisitiveness. People, instead of deeply exploring the unknown, try to quickly wind-up a study so they can publish. Or, even worse, many try to work on projects that have predictable 'best' outcomes that can be published in a 'reputed' journal.

Two, the mismatch in the level of inquisitiveness between the supervisor and the student is a common cause for the student being fired or forced to quit. When the supervisor or the guide has a higher level of inquisitiveness, the students feel overburdened. They feel they are under pressure all the time and how much ever they do, the supervisor always has something more to say. In my opinion, most of the cases (obviously not all) deal with the over-inquisitiveness of the supervisor and the lack of enough inquisitiveness in the student. Imagine a professor very interested in research but couldn't spend enough time in research due to teaching and other administrative activities. He is so eager to know what the current study going in the lab would lead to. When the student reports a result, his/her mind goes back into the experimental procedure done by the student and forward into the result obtained. He/she asks a number of questions as to why it is done in a particular way and why not the other way? Why is it measured this way and not the other way? What if the data is interpreted differently? If the student is really inquisitive enough, he would have thought on those lines already and would have an answer. If not, the student feels overwhelmed.

If you are a doctoral student and facing this situation, change your perspective that the supervisor is very demanding! Have a perspective that your supervisor is over-inquisitive, which is good! He/she is so eager to know the next outcome that when their inquisitiveness is not kindled or satisfied, they feel you are under-performing! The only solution is to naturally develop inquisitiveness, else you will quit! All of us understand that every individual is unique and many wouldn't want to be inquisitive but rather do things they already know to earn a living and live peacefully than always being anxious about the outcome of what they do! Perfectly fine! And that's one reason why a PhD isn't for everybody!

I have seen it happen the other way too! The student is very inquisitive and wants to do / try a lot of things but the lack of inquisitiveness in the Professor creates conflicts. And that's why choosing your supervisor is such a huge and defining step of your PhD!

Keeps your brain active!

PhD is not time-bound, if somebody says you can work on your PhD just from 9 AM to 5 PM, 5 days a week for 4 years, don't believe it! It is not a 9 AM – 5 PM job! Even if you go home by 5 PM every day, your mind will revolve around your research. You will be constantly thinking of how to tackle the current challenge or what is the right way to express or interpret the observation. While some see it as not healthy and pressurizing (which is true for many), taken in the right sense and done in the right way, it keeps your brain active! An idle mind is a devil's workshop, rest assured that your mind wouldn't be idle when you do a PhD!

Some still wonder how this can be a healthy trend? We talk so much about work-life balance and is it good to think about work all the time? I will give a few analogies. A child will be thinking about their play time that day and will be so much looking forward to going to the play area the next day! A groom will look forward to the day of wedding much eagerly! You may ask how does that compare with work? Just as a child enjoys playing and a groom eagerly awaits the day of wedding, researchers love (or should love) doing research! PhD is for those who belong to this category who would enjoy doing research and knowing the unknown! In fact, this is the secret behind the smiling faces at work! Many people fail to figure out what they enjoy doing and live a miserable life doing things that would fetch money but not real happiness!

> *"Many people fail to figure out what they enjoy doing and live a miserable life doing things that would fetch money but not real happiness!*
>
> *- Vijayavenkataraman Sanjairaj"*

If you are thinking of doing a PhD, introspect yourself to see if you are 'inquisitive' enough and if you will really enjoy doing research! If you find that is the case, no matter the obstacles that you face during or after your PhD, you will enjoy what you have done (are doing), never regret the decision of taking up a PhD, and you will definitely go on to finish your PhD with flying colors!

> *"If you are thinking of doing a PhD, introspect yourself to see if you are 'inquisitive' enough and if you will really enjoy doing research! If you find that is the case, no matter the obstacles that you face*

during or after your PhD, you will enjoy what you have done (are doing), never regret the decision of taking up a PhD, and you will definitely go on to finish your PhD with flying colors!

- Vijayavenkataraman Sanjairaj **"**

Other perks

There are a lot of other perks in doing a PhD! A PhD in a foreign country will be a gateway for you to live in the land of your dream! While a Master's degree itself can accomplish this goal, many choose PhD because a PhD pays them but a Master's requires them to pay! The salary that a graduate will get in his/her country will be half of the stipend that a PhD will pay! These scenarios depend on which country you come from and which country you go for doing your PhD!

Travel opportunities are a huge perk that accompanies PhD! Conferences are gateways to travel and many consider them to be 'glorified vacations'! Both yes and no! For some, hearing and knowing the latest in their field from other experts itself is so gratifying while for others travelling to a different country is the main motivation! Either way, your knowledge expands, your worldview changes as you travel and mingle with peers from different countries and cultures! Your prejudices will (hopefully) come down!

I personally have seen many who fall in the trap of joining a PhD for other 'instrumental' benefits or perks such as a higher stipend than they get in a company in their country, considering it a gateway of entering a country of their dream, being called a 'Dr', opportunities for travel, etc. Yes, these are perks and will be perks only if you 'fit in' to the basic framework of being inquisitive and enjoy doing research!

> *"I personally have seen many who fall in the trap of joining a PhD for other 'instrumental' benefits or perks such as a higher stipend than they get in a company in their country, considering it a gateway of entering a country of their dream, being called a 'Dr', opportunities for travel, etc. Yes, these are perks and will be perks only if you 'fit in' to the basic framework of being inquisitive and enjoy doing research!*
>
> *- Vijayavenkataraman Sanjairaj"*

CHAPTER IV

Is a PhD for me? Personalizing PhD

There is always a personal element in doing a PhD. You might have all the qualifications (read academic standing and passion) to pursue a PhD but the circumstances might not be just right. You might think you can successfully survive the PhD but your introspection might be illusive ('introspection illusion'). Or you might have missed assessing your capability and ability in its full sense. I am not going to talk in detail about the right introspection techniques or capability/ability matrix but rather talk about a few practical points to consider.

Capability vs Ability

There is a subtle difference between capability and ability. While you might be capable of doing a PhD, given your situation, you may not be able to take it up. It is important to not only assess your capability but also your ability. There are many points to consider, a few of the most important ones:

1. Personality traits
2. Financial aspects
3. Family commitment
4. Future plans

Personality traits

PhD requires working under stress and tight deadlines. Introspect yourself to see if you are a person who would take that as a challenge and work to succeed. Not having a PhD is not a crime, you could still do research without a PhD. I know a researcher who works for a particular professor as a research assistant for more than 8 years. I was a PhD student then and I asked her 'Why not take up a PhD?'. She said she can't manage the time stress that comes with PhD and publication pressure. She is happy assisting the PhD students and postdocs in the lab in their research and lab management.

> *"Not having a PhD is not a crime, you could still do research without a PhD.*
>
> *-Vijayavenkataraman Sanjairaj"*

She leads individual projects but without tight deadlines. Your personality traits play a major role. Take time to talk to people who have done and who are doing PhD in the field you are interested in, from the lab/school that you are aiming for, introspect yourself to see if you fit in to the requirements and your ability to adapt to the challenging environment.

Financial Aspects

PhD costs money! When you aim for a PhD, aim for good schools or good labs, the best however would be a good lab at a good school. There are people who desperately want to do a PhD and end up falling prey to schools/PhD programs that are not accredited. Though I personally don't know anybody in that category, I have read posts in social media and news media about many of these innocent lots! One easy way to judge if the program is good is that PhD would be free and it will pay you a stipend! Almost all of the non-accredited schools or programs exist to monger money and you can be quite sure that you have to reconsider your decision if you are asked to pay a tuition fee, diploma fee, exam fee, enrollment fee, etc.

Does that mean good schools don't charge any of the fees for the PhD? They do! But you get a scholarship. The scholarship works differently in different countries. The type of scholarship could broadly be classified into three:

i.   *Government or institutional scholarship:* In Singapore, for example, the PhD scholarship comes from the government/institution and each Professor will have a quota of PhD students under this scholarship. In New York University Abu Dhabi, there is a global PhD fellowship sponsored by the institution.

ii. *Professor's research grant:* In the US and many of the European countries, the PhD students are hired from externally funded research grants. Professors, individually or as a collaborative group apply to external funds to government agencies such as National Science Foundation (NSF) and National Institutes of Health (NIH) in the US, European Research Council (ERC) in European Union, Swiss NSF in Switzerland OR private funding agencies (research foundations / societies) OR industries.

iii. *External PhD Fellowships/Scholarships:* The funding for PhD comes from an industry in collaboration with a university (many a times supported/co-funded by the government). Many such PhD programs are now offered in Europe and the UK (e.g. WASP Industrial PhD program in Sweden, Industrial PhD by Innovation Fund

Denmark, Industrial doctorate program at University of Strathclyde, etc.). There are a host of other external PhD fellowships (partial and full-funding) including the commonwealth scholarships, Rhodes scholarships, Gates Cambridge Scholarship, Fullbright program, The Hertz foundation, etc. Please note that the eligibility conditions of these scholarships may vary based on your citizenship, field of study, etc.

If you have enough money to spend, you don't have to worry about the financial aspects of a PhD! But it is very rare to see self-funded PhDs! When you look out for a PhD, keep these things in mind. The quantum of funding and scholarship varies from country to country, program to program, school to school and between different fellowships. Depending on your personal situation, choose the country and fellowship wisely! More on the country of choice in the next chapter. For example, if you are a master's graduate, working for a company in the R&D division, an industrial PhD is definitely the best option. You don't have to resign your current job nor jump into some new field of research and best of all you get a tertiary degree as you work in the industry with a promised future.

Family Commitments

PhD is a long-term commitment and it is intense! Taking into account the family commitments is absolutely necessary and important. If you are still single and unmarried, nothing like that! Ask a PhD student, he/she will tell you they are first "married to their PhD". Managing a family and PhD is not impossible but may be strenuous. I am not coming to say that you cannot do a PhD if you have a family, no, not at all! All I say is take that into consideration. Even single and unmarried guys may have dependent parents care for.

> *"PhD is a long-term commitment and it is intense! Taking into account the family commitments is absolutely necessary and important.*
>
> *-Vijayavenkataraman Sanjairaj"*

Take into consideration both the financial commitment to the family and the time commitment. PhD stipends might not be enough to support a family (may be enough and it depends on the quality of life you live, spending behavior, etc.). If you are married and your spouse is also working, it might take care of the financial part but again you might have additional expenses such as having a maid or caretaker to maintain the home or take care of your aging/aged parents or blooming kids. The second important aspect is the time. Most PhDs are intense and require a significant amount of time every day. Even when you go home, you might be overwhelmed with thoughts about your PhD work! Not only the time spent with your family is limited but also the quality of time. Be well-prepared to tackle time. How to balance your time effectively is the key to simultaneously succeed in your PhD and the family!

> *"Be well-prepared to tackle time. How to balance your time effectively is the key to simultaneously succeed in your PhD and the family!*
>
> *- Vijayavenkataraman Sanjairaj"*

If you are a single child and your parents are aged, they might feel very lonely if you go to a foreign country to do a PhD, with the frequency of travel to home being once or at most twice a year! The feeling is very common in Asian countries. Though the parents will be proud of their children, the feeling of loneliness still remains! To those family-oriented people (like me), consider choosing a school/country close to home. I am from India and I chose Singapore. It's a 4 hours flight from home but still you get a world class PhD!

Future long-term Plans

Planning your PhD is planning your future! Although you can't plan 100% of your future, at least think of which country you want to settle in. Are you going abroad just for your PhD and planning to return back home? Think about the prospects after you return. Will you be overqualified for jobs at home? Are you planning to settle in the country where you want to do your PhD? If so, what are the job prospects in that country? Are you thinking of doing your PhD in one country but then relocating to another country (maybe you got a very good scholarship in a particular country that you don't want to miss but you don't plan to be in the country long-term)? In that case, how is the PhD valued in the country of your future?

You may also have to consider the family aspects into your future plans. Does the country where you do a PhD give resident rights to your spouse? Most of the countries might have a minimum cap of salary to bring in your dependents. You have to check if the PhD stipend satisfies that criterion. Do you have dependent parents that you wish to take with you after your PhD? There are only a handful of countries (like Australia and Canada) that have a system to give permanent residency to the dependent parents (of course, subject to a lot of terms and conditions).

While accurate planning of the future is not possible, it is good to consider and keep in mind the long-term financial aspects and family commitments before you decide to pursue a PhD.

> *"While accurate planning of the future is not possible, it is good to consider and keep in mind the long-term financial aspects and family commitments before you decide to pursue a PhD.*
>
> *-Vijayavenkataraman Sanjairaj"*

CHAPTER V

Which country should I go to?

A major decision that will affect your present and future will be the country of choice to pursue your PhD. Most people prefer going to the US or Western Europe and Australia for their PhD, while Asian students are increasingly considering many other countries such as Singapore, China, Hong Kong, Taiwan, South Korea, Japan, and Israel. Though uncommon, students from the US and Europe also consider doing their PhD in the Asian and African continents, more so for their field trips, especially in the fields of arts, humanities, and social sciences. It is heart-warning to see this vast cultural exchange and globalization. Depending on the field of research and resource availability, each country has its own unique offerings. Leaving aside the academic part of it, there are other practical things to consider, which I will talk about in this chapter.

There are a number of factors that you should consider before choosing where to do your PhD:

1. Financial Aspects including taxation
2. Family values in the context of culture
3. Future long-term plans

Financial Aspects including taxation

In the last article, I talked about the financial aspects to consider before deciding to do a PhD. If and once you have decided to pursue it, the other financial aspects during and after your PhD should be considered into your application process.

The first and foremost will be the stipend (or salary) that you would get as a PhD student. The amount varies drastically between countries. Keeping in mind your family commitments and your standard of living, you should evaluate if you could live comfortably with the amount of stipend or salary that you receive. Some wonder why it is 'stipend' OR 'salary'! I will address it in the next paragraph! Now, as of 2021, as I write this chapter, the average stipend or salary that a PhD student gets in the US is 20k to 30k USD per annum, 25k to 30k CAD per annum in Canada, 25k to 30k GBP per annum in the UK, 3k to 4k EUR per month in Germany, 2k to 3k SGD per month in Singapore and 50k to 150k JPY per month in Japan. These are just average values and a simple google search will give you exhaustive information on the subject. Consider the amount and compare it with your current or calculated monthly / yearly expenses to decide whether the amount you get would be comfortable to manage yourself and other family commitments.

Second, I kept mentioning 'stipend' or 'salary' because different modes of PhD funding in the same country and different countries consider the amount paid to a PhD student either as a stipend or salary or both! For example, in the US, if the source of PhD funding is a scholarship award, it is tax-free while the teaching assistantships are taxable. In Germany, the PhD funding is considered a salary and is taxable. This is a very important consideration because taxes differ from country to country and it may be as high as 20 or 30%. Do clarify whether you receive a stipend or a salary! When you consider your expenses and savings, consider your income after tax! To many who consider doing a PhD, this might be an easy filter to decide whether it is financially sustainable to pursue a PhD in a particular country.

Thirdly, consider the post-PhD opportunities and salaries in the countries of your choice. What are the opportunities and salary range in the country of study, if you are planning to settle for a long-term? You might be single when you start your PhD and might have a family during or after your study. Explore if the opportunities and salary are good enough to manage a family?

Family values in the context of culture

While financial aspects are important, they are not all! There is much more to consider in life than just money! The first consideration would be to know if the country where you think you can do your PhD allows your family to be with you during your PhD, if you have a family. We have seen this point in the last chapter. What many miss considering is the family values in the context of culture. While it is easy for a bachelor or spinster to adapt to the new culture, the scenario is totally different when it comes to raising kids in a foreign country. If you are not planning to be a chronic bachelor and foresee wedding your love of life, consider the environment in which you want to bring up your kids in.

I can talk about a lot of specific examples but I will give a generic example here. I come from a traditional South Indian family background. Many of my friends from similar family backgrounds and values live abroad. I interact with them and give counseling to most of them. One theme that keeps repeating is the 'identification crisis' that the next generation goes through in a foreign land. I will explain. Mr. X goes to the US to pursue his graduate studies, does very well and was placed in a very good position. His long-term plan is to settle in the US. He is more than comfortable living abroad and has adapted to the new environment. He still holds to his family traditions and values, be it the type of food he eats, alcohol consumption, or other rituals if any. He has a choice and he sticks to it (nothing right or wrong!). Luckily, he (or his parents mostly) finds the love of his life, Ms Y, having similar family values and outlook on life. They were happily married! Life goes on and brings in joy, baby Z, the little bundle of love was born. Baby Z grows up, and it is time for schooling now. As Z grows up, he or she will face an 'identity crisis' in their teenage years. The family (parents and grand-parents) teaches and practices a set of cultural values. While at School, they have to deal with a completely different set of cultural values. And tragically, most of the time, they are contrary and conflicting to each other! I will give a specific example which I heard in a talk show. A 25-year-old girl of Indian origin took her life away as she was not allowed to have a boyfriend! Why? Her parents are from a traditional south Indian background and they think having a boyfriend is a taboo. The girl goes through a lot of stress in her high school and college/university where not having a boyfriend is being mocked at. She couldn't manage the conflicting themes and was torn between the two spheres, went on to take an extremely stupid decision to take her life away! What a tragedy Mr.X and Ms. Y had to face! They have everything but they lost their only child!

My intention is not to scare you but prepare you. There are so many who are doing well abroad, blending into the different cultures. I personally know many Indians from similar backgrounds who are happily married to foreigners, bringing up their children in the family values of both the sides of the parents, giving them different cultural contexts and perspectives. The point is, have you thought about it and are you prepared for it? This is not something unique to south India, I have personally seen this cultural identity crisis in other nationalities too! Chinese, Singaporeans, Malaysians, Europeans and Americans! While some are mature enough to handle these, some are not. Better safe than sorry!

While it may not be such a big consideration to some people, this might be so important to others! I leave it to the discretion of the readers as to how important this aspect is, depending on their background, family and cultural settings.

Future long-term Plans

We talked so much about the family scenarios, which brings in the next factor of your future long-term plans. Are you planning to settle in that country in the long-run? Have you considered all the financial aspects and family values? What are your financial goals and personal goals? Will the country that you choose to invest your time and energy for your PhD be suitable and supportive of your goals?

Like I always say, life is full of surprises. It is not humanly possible to draft a complete and perfect future plan. There will be deviations, twists and turns but it would be foolish not to plan the future at all. Give some thoughts to your future plans, consider multiple options, think of plan B's, and worst-case scenarios. I am sure it will prepare you mentally for things that come your way in the future!

"Like I always say, life is full of surprises. It is not humanly possible to draft a complete and perfect future plan. There will be deviations, there will be twists and turns but it would be foolish not to plan the future at all.

-Vijayavenkataraman Sanjairaj"

Which university should I choose?

Having considered all the points mentioned in the last chapter about choosing a country (or countries), the next big question would be 'Which University should I choose?'. I will give a few practical tips on choosing the right University:

1. Choose the 'best' University (Obvious? ☺)
2. Choose the 'best' lab
3. Best University vs best lab?

Choose the 'best' University

When it comes to choosing the universities, choose the best always! While it seems to be very obvious, the 'best' always varies according to the individual's situation and perception. First, qualify yourself to get into the world's best universities. There are so many international rankings of universities that are published every year. Although many have their reservations of these rankings (more emphasis on research and less emphasis on teaching OR the criteria of evaluation, etc.), let us accept the fact that there will always be a best list! Try getting into one of them! With the increasing competition, students who did their undergraduates in such institutions stand a higher chance of getting a graduate admission. Yet, there are so many from different countries, who did their undergraduate degrees in not so well-known institutions, worked hard (and smart), climbed their way through all odds and secured admissions in the world's best institutions! What is important is to prepare yourself for the same, notwithstanding the educational background you come from. Two key qualifications that could better your chances are publications and language. You may be an undergraduate student or a Master's student or a graduate working in an industry considering a PhD, work with a professor in the field of your interest, not only to gain experience but also possible publications. I always encourage my undergraduate students to be part of our research projects and include them in the publications as co-authors and I also give them a long-term project that could lead to a first-author publication. The second qualification is the language. Many might wonder why? The most important aspect of research is communication. If you can't write or talk about your research in a language that another scientist or a layman can understand, there is little use of your research. You must have the right words and sentences, the nuances of the language, to communicate your ideas and results clearly! Now, you might think I am only talking about English. True, English has become the *lingua franca* in the scientific and the broader academic field. It is not just about English. If you plan to do your PhD in Germany, learning German can be of immense help. Knowing German can lead you to more fruitful discussions with the native speakers as they may find at ease conversing in their mother tongue! Another aspect of language is to develop communicating the complex research jargons in simple terms that would appeal to the masses.

"The most important aspect of research is communication. If you can't write or talk about your research in a language that another scientist or a layman can understand, there is little use of your research. You must have the right words and sentences, the nuances of the language, to communicate your ideas and results clearly!

-Vijayavenkataraman Sanjairaj"

We have talked enough about the best universities and the two key qualifications that would better prepare you for the same! Now, I come to the next philosophical observation. What's best to the world might not be best to you! Define what is 'best' to you! This thought is on the similar lines of 'personalizing your PhD'. You might be particularly interested in pursuing your higher education in a specific country or a specific university, which might not appear in the world's best list but is highly respectable in your culture. It might also be for family reasons. I have heard from some families that through four generations, they have attended the same University and they bask in that fact! When you personalize your PhD using the tips I mentioned in that article, you also define, in tandem, the 'best' list of universities from your perspective. Define it and prepare for it!

"What's best to the world might not be best to you! Define what is 'best' to you!

-Vijayavenkataraman Sanjairaj"

Choose the best lab/group

There is another approach to choosing the University, that is to choose the best lab/group! By best lab, I mean the best department or literally the best lab/group (doing pioneer research in the field). I will give a specific example for better understanding. Per the Times Higher Education ranking 2020, Rice University in the US stands at rank 105 globally but they have one of the best bioengineering departments in the world! If a student considers a PhD in Bioengineering, he/she could choose Rice University on par with the top 50 world universities (just a qualitative comparison). Do a thorough study of your field of interest, research outputs and innovations; define the 'best' in your field and go for it. The rankings also might come in handy, as they give field-specific (department-specific) global rankings too!

One of the best ways to evaluate a particular department or a lab is to see the quality of their research. I will talk more about it in the next chapter on choosing the right professor but just a snippet here. Go to the department or the lab websites, look at the many projects that they work on, their publications, their translational research, the research infrastructure, and where the students go after graduation! Infrastructure is key! Do check out if the list of equipment that you would commonly use for the research is available in the department / lab and the real availability for you to use. If you are still in doubt, look out for the 'open house' programme of the department or university, which would definitely have a 'lab tour' component. Talk with your friends (or friend's friends, acquaintances, or even strangers) working in the department or the lab to get insights into the working environment. All these strategies will give you a wealth of information that would help you make your decision for or against the department or the lab.

Best university vs best group

The first choice, in my opinion, will be the best group in the best university. This would not only add value to your CV but also a tremendous research experience. This is the best-case scenario and if you achieve it, congratulations! If you don't or have a dilemma between choosing the best university vs best lab, do a thorough analysis of the pros and cons of both the options. I will give an example.

Scenario 1: You are interested in a research field 'A'. You did your research and found a group in the world's best university who also work mainly on field 'A'. This is an excellent match and a perfect fit! Go ahead, prepare yourself to get into your dream group!

Scenario 2: You are interested in a research field 'A'. You did your research and found a group in the world's best university who work on field 'A' but field 'A' is not the main focus of the group. You might have found another group at a different university, lower in rank than the former, but the group's main focus is field 'A'. The most difficult scenario is where you have to carefully weigh the pros and cons. It is very subjective and I don't go to give a rubric of assessing the same but do not ignore this step before you zero in on a particular university.

Scenario 3: You are interested in a research field 'A'. You did your research and found the best group (the university might not be featuring in the top 50 or 100). If you are confident that your experience in that group is going to be great, have no second thoughts, go for it!

In addition to all the above points, also consider the support mechanisms available in the department and

University for developing skills other than research, which are very important for the future career, be it in academia or industry. Look for and consider active University-Industry collaborations that would not only lead to internships or secondments but also aid in doing translational research. And last but not least, take into account the undergraduate-level teaching and mentoring opportunities.

Some might think of it as a rat race! Going for the best universities or best groups, running behind paper degrees or vainglory! I will give you two perspectives of it.

The first: Don't consider it a rat race, consider it a pursuit of excellence. Excellence is subjective and should be custom-defined by each individual. You are not running after the conventions of the world or the majority but rather seeking for a fruitful research experience. The fruitfulness will definitely depend on the research environment, facilities, quality of people and quality of work. These are extensively considered in the global rankings and that's why it could give you guidance (not the ultimatum!).

The second: If you have the means of breaking the convention, be it skills or financial means, you always have a choice! Many innovators in the world do not hold a PhD, rather they employ PhDs to execute their ideas! Do you think you have a great idea for research that can change the world but you don't have the so-called paper-based or number-based qualifications to enter the best university? Never mind, be brave enough to work on your ideas, keep knocking and the door will definitely be opened!

CHAPTER VII

Choosing the right professor

If there is one person other than you and one factor other than the choice of university that would determine the success of your PhD, that would be the Professor! PhD is a long-term (and most of the time, a life-time) commitment where the Professor (Supervisor)-Student relationship is very critical! There are academic family trees where you will be identified with your professor long after you finish your PhD! Given the importance of this relationship, choosing the right Professor (for you!) is such an important decision that should be taken with a lot of wisdom!

No human is perfect, including Professors! Now, I hear someone murmuring that their professor is inhuman! Ahem, I better condone the murmur and move on. Each individual has a personality and it is important to select someone with whom our 'chemistry' would work! Depending on your personality and what you want to achieve, choose the group and the Professor wisely. Though I cannot go to list all the personality types and ask you to do psychometric tests for the Professor and group members, I will talk about a few generic personality types and group dynamics that might help you in the process of choosing your supervisor.

"If there is one person other than you and one factor other than the choice of university that would determine the success of your PhD, that would be the Professor! PhD is a long-term (and most of the time, a life-time) commitment where the Professor

(Supervisor)-Student relationship is very critical!
-Vijayavenkataraman Sanjairaj"

Big group vs small group

Before I move on to the personality of the professors, let us talk about the size of the group and its impact. Some groups are really big, having anywhere between 50-100 people, including the senior postdocs, post-docs, PhD students and other graduate students. On the other hand, many groups have modest numbers within 10, having 2 or 3 post-docs, 2 or 3 PhD students and a couple of other graduate students. Both big and small groups have their own pros and cons. Depending on your personality, you might fit into either of them. I will talk about a few pros and cons of both to give you hints before you make a choice.

Big groups usually enjoy good funding, a lot of projects in the pipeline and an opportunity to work with a variety of projects and people. You will not only have the depth of the project but also a breadth of related projects. However, there might be several limitations (well, depends on you) as well. Given the sheer number, the equipment availability for each individual might be an issue. Most of the time, you will have to primarily work with a postdoc for your PhD and your interaction with your PhD Supervisor might be minimal. I have seen cases where the chemistry between the postdoc in-charge and the PhD student spoiled and the PhD student has to go through a lot of struggles. Another point to consider is that you might end up with a large number of publications (which is important and is good) by a small contribution in terms of the experiments or data analysis which might make you lose your focus on your 'prime' contribution. In other words, you might be too used to working in large groups and getting easy help that if you want to start working individually later during your postdoc, you might feel the heat. I am talking about cases here and this is not the norm but like I always say, better be prepared for the worst-case scenario.

Small group, on the other hand, gives a lot of mentoring time with the Professor. Your individual contribution will become very important and you will be forced to learn and operate a variety of equipment that would be useful in the long run. In terms of cons, if the Professor is micromanaging and your personality type doesn't suit, that will be a huge problem. You can't even avoid him/her as the group size is too small and limited external help as there will only be a couple of post-docs. Successful PhDs come out of both the types of groups even as you are reading! Think of these points beforehand so that you will be well-prepared to start your PhD journey.

Supervisor and Co-supervisor

More interdisciplinary the type of PhD topics become, there is an increasing trend to have two supervisors, specializing in different areas. While this is good, the relationship between the two supervisors will play a role in determining how smooth your PhD journey would be! I had two supervisors and I was glad I had two! They were for each other and I have never seen any contradictions between them. If the position that you are taking is associated with two groups, it is always good to talk to the students beforehand to understand the dynamics!

Self-learning vs directed-learning

There are many different types of groups and supervisors. The first generic group I can think of is self-learning vs directed learning. There are certain groups where you are left to decide on your PhD topic, the progress, and the means of doing it. While some may think it is horrendous, I am of the opposite view! I did such a PhD and I was completely satisfied with it! I had a lot of learning and it was a very fruitful and valuable experience! Of course, it was a lot of hard work and long nights, nevertheless, the most fruitful of my career so far! But it will not suit everybody. Some may require or prefer directed-learning, where the project is already there and there are people to help and guide in every step. There would be clear objectives to achieve and a clear path to traverse, of course laden with uncertainties and surprises. Depending on your personality type, evaluate which type of group or Professor will fit you well. Current staff and students can give you the most valuable inside information.

Assistant, Associate, and Full Professor

One criterion to consider is also the academic title of the PhD supervisor. Assistant Professors will have a lot of time for you, as you are an important part of their career and your achievement and their achievements are intertwined. This also means that you will have a lot of attention and sometimes a little more pressure. Full professors are established in their research field and might be burdened with many administrative works, your time with them might be limited. Associate Professors are somewhere in between. Again, some might prefer a very pushy Assistant

Professor, that they would learn and do a lot within a short amount of time while some others would prefer established full professors to learn and glean from their experience. This is just a generic guideline and doesn't mean all Assistant Professors will be pushy and all full Professors will not have enough time for their PhD students. A lot of other factors like availability of a senior post-doc in the group or the structure of the PhD program will also play a role in balancing the PhD experience as a whole. Again, the current staff and students can give you the most valuable inside information.

Milestones vs Micromanagement

There are professors who set milestones and will not disturb you until that time. They might inquire of you periodically to check if you are progressing in the right direction to achieve that milestone. There are others who might do micromanagement. They want to know what you do every day and expect an update. I have seen both approaches and though I personally love the milestone-based approach, there were people who benefitted from the micromanagement as they would know exactly what to do next. When I was doing my PhD, I knew of a professor who would call my fellow PhD student every day and talk for an hour. They did not have any regular weekly or biweekly meetings but individual updates every day! Though that was pressurizing for my friend, he ended up with a long-list of impactful publications and a secured future. And that professor was an Assistant Professor ☺.

Effort-oriented vs results-oriented

There is another generic distinction between the personality of the professors that I could think of. Some are effort-oriented while some are results-oriented. I will explain with examples. There was a professor I know of in Singapore and whom I have collaborated with during my PhD, whose criteria for his PhD student's graduation is very simple, 4 research papers in decent journals. Seems pretty straight-forward, right? Despite all odds, they have to achieve the goal. He will do his best to provide the infrastructure but the learning and progress is the student's responsibility. I know many of his students, some appreciate this approach and went on to do well later in their academic career while some couldn't achieve the goal (for genuine reasons not of student's fault) and did not get to submit their PhD thesis for graduation for 7 years (but went on to do well in a very reputed company, that's a different story! ☺). There are other professors who would value your efforts and learning throughout the process rather than just the result (publication or others). As long as they are confident that you have done enough for your PhD in terms of knowledge contribution, whether it is published or not, they might allow you to graduate. If you get a professor, who is both, who is interested in the results but also cares deeply about your efforts, nothing like it, go for him/her!

How do I know or evaluate the group or the Professor?

The best way is to get inside information from the current students and staff! Talk to people and understand the dynamics of both the Professor and the group! Be careful in your evaluation, don't take everything that is told to you as such. Do your analysis! What someone might hate might be just the thing that you are looking for in a group or a professor! If you are a current undergraduate or Master's student, the other best way is to volunteer to be part of the research group (student volunteers, research assistant, research intern, summer intern, etc.) to learn first-hand and evaluate if it would be the right environment for you to do your PhD. If you are a graduate and considering doing a PhD, apply for research assistant positions to evaluate both your interest in doing a PhD if that would suit you and also the Professor or group that you are interested in!

Now that I have written so much, this is not all. And there is no one blanket rule or criteria to select a professor and intellectually, I don't see a point in telling only one approach is right (e.g., milestones over micromanagement). What I emphasize is that each one is different and what is best for one might not be the best for another! What will work for one will not work for another! Assess your personality well, talk to people from the group, talk to the Professor himself, evaluate your suitability if you will fit in well with the group dynamics and make a wise decision. I emphasize wisdom here as this relationship is a life-time relationship and many times it might be emotional too! Choose a one who will mentor you for life and will serve as a role-model for you and your career! Choose the one whom you think you can trust! Choose the one who is genuinely caring and concerned deeply about you and your career! I know it might be hard and tedious but if you find one, you are one of the luckiest people!

"*Choose a one who will mentor you for life and will serve as a role-model for you and your career! Choose the one whom you think you can trust! Choose the one who is genuinely caring and concerned deeply about you and your career! I know it might be hard and tedious but if you find one, you are one of the luckiest people!*

-Vijayavenkataraman Sanjairaj"

CHAPTER VIII

Choosing the right thesis topic

We have already seen the importance and tips of choosing the right country, university, and professor. We will now move on to another important choice before any PhD aspirant, the topic of their thesis and how to choose it wisely. I feel many PhD aspirants do not give importance to their choice of thesis topic as much as they give for the country / university / professor. While choosing a professor somewhat defines your thesis area, choosing the thesis topic, according to me, is more than that! I will tell you why I think so:

1. Your thesis topic will stay with you for life in your CV or resume, throughout your career!
2. Your thesis topic, to a greater extent, determines your early career years where you have limited flexibility to change your field.
3. If you choose your thesis topic wisely, you could go on working on it for life, throughout your career and of course, building on and around it!

I will talk about a few options that might be before you, the importance of it and a few tips on how to choose between them.

Applying for a PhD position with a detailed project description

Many of the US and European universities will have open PhD positions with detailed project descriptions. These project descriptions will talk about the background of the field, the challenges involved and what will the project solve aka goals of the project. Most commonly, the professor or a group of researchers have been granted funding from the government or other non-governmental agencies to work on a specific project and the PhD positions offered are part of this project. In a way, it is easier for the student as they have their project goals defined already, the skills required for the project are known and can be learnt and it would be a smooth start. If you are someone who find it difficult to decide on a particular topic (you must anyway have a strong preference of what field you would want yourself to be in already – e.g., renewable energy, biosensors, water research, roman architecture, etc.), this is a good option for you. However, somebody else (the Professor or the group of researchers) have already 'thought' on your behalf and you will have limited leeway in working on your own ideas as the project goals, deliverables, and deadlines are already fixed! You can, however, bring your ideas on how to execute the project to achieve the desired goal. If you are someone who already has a passion on a particular field and you would want a little leeway to explore and find your passion, then this option might not be the right one for you! You could try the next option!

Applying for a PhD position in a field of your interest

There are other PhD positions that are offered as a scholarship or fellowship and it doesn't come from a specific project grant. With these PhD positions, you will have freedom to navigate within the scope of your professor's research. For example, I work on Additive manufacturing and bioprinting for tissue engineering and other biomedical applications. My PhD students are admitted through an institutional PhD Fellowship and I always give them the freedom to choose a thesis topic / area within the broader field of my research. In fact, I encourage my students to do a thorough literature review of the sub-topics they are interested in, and come up with their 'own' ideas which I would then chip in and carve to make it a niche field. For example, it could be a new bioprinting method overcoming the challenges with the current techniques, it could be on novel bioprintable materials, it could also be using the current bioprinting methods and biomaterials but to address a specific disease condition or a specific tissue. I give that time for all my students to figure out but some students might not find their topic of passion and they come back to me asking for suggestions, I guide them by giving more clues pointing to the sub-discipline that they could work on and after several meetings and discussions, finalize a topic that is of interest to both the group in general and to the student in specific! If it is just of interest to the Professor and the group and not to the student, the student can't stand 4 or 5 years doing 'valuable' research in that field!

Most of the professors will be interested in allowing you to pursue a new sub-topic within their field, without much diversion from their core area of research. Do not write to a Professor of Engineering and express your interest in pursuing research on art history! I know nobody would make such an obvious mistake but the many emails that I get everyday actually tells me people can actually do this mistake out of desperation in getting a position! I get emails from people who had done their Masters and even PhD (those applying for postdoc positions) in a completely different area and seeking a position in my lab, without even mentioning how they could use their skills or align within the scope of my research. I cannot help but ignore such emails!

If you already have an idea that you want to explore, write to or discuss with the Professors your idea and get their suggestions. You might think it is an idea worth pursuing but the Professors might not! It could turn out both ways! The first is that you are new to the field and the Professors being experienced and having constant touch with the experts in the field, they might be right! Don't be adamant that your ideas are the best and it will definitely work. Try to get as much feedback and inputs as possible and shape / change / carve your ideas accordingly. The second is that the Professors might be wrong in thinking that your idea might not work! There might be various reasons, their core area of research might be different and the idea that you are proposing is an application of their core expertise where they might lack expertise, some might not have kept themselves up with the advancements in the field or even worse, their ego might prevent them from accepting your idea as novel or workable! I mean it and I have seen so many students suffer! If you are confident that your idea will work, talk to more people who align with your thoughts and support your ideas.

Topics of basic research or applied research or of industrial relevance

In one of the points, I mentioned above on the importance of choosing the right thesis topic, I mentioned the impact of your thesis topic on your early career. It is always good to have an idea of where you want to get after your PhD, academia or industry? While some may be clear, some may not be able to decide this early on, I understand. Think of all the other factors including your family and financial needs, getting any kind of job that would sustain you and your family might be the priority for many! If that is the case, think of the varied opportunities that you could get into after your PhD. I will give an example. Being a Professor of Engineering, I couldn't avoid giving examples from the same field, bear with me if you are arts or history majors! Doing a PhD on the topic of batteries would open up your opportunities to a wide range of industries including automobile industry (with the increased adoption of clean electric vehicles). Think and compare if you do a PhD on the topic of biomass gasification. Both are in the same field of energy but the former might increase your range of options post-PhD. Now, that doesn't mean those who work on biomass gasification are low in the rank. They do a wonderful service to the environment and they could tune their research towards production and storage of hydrogen from biomass, which would be a huge hit! All I want to impress upon you is that be wise in choosing your thesis topic!

To give you tips on choosing, think whether you want to work on basic research, applied research or topics of industrial relevance! Basic research is much needed, unlike some giving undue importance to only applied research. How many of you know that the Professor who wanted to study the 'extremophiles' (organisms living in extreme conditions) in the hot springs at the Yellowstone National

Park was mocked at first! A new bacterium, named *thermus aquaticus*, was identified that could thrive even at 70 degrees Celsius! Any idea how that is helping the world now in 2021? The enzymes from that bacterium that could survive higher temperatures is the key ingredient in the PCR (Polymerase Chain Reaction) tests that are considered the gold-standard for testing the COVID virus!

So, be it basic, applied or topics of industrial relevance, you are working to change the world! Just think of which one might suit you and your needs better and give your best in whatever you choose!

> "*Be it basic, applied or topics of industrial relevance, when you do your PhD, you are working to change the world! Just think of which one might suit you and your needs better and give your best in whatever you choose!*
>
> *-Vijayavenkataraman Sanjairaj*"

CHAPTER IX

How do I start (my PhD)?

All that has been said and done so far is just a prelude of what to come! If you had already chosen the country, the group, and the Professor and have committed to do a PhD, Congratulations! The real work starts now. There are many things that need your focus in the first few months (sometimes the whole first year). I have divided them into the following subsections:

1. Focus on your Coursework
2. Do a thorough literature review
3. Identify the gaps – novelty stems out of it!
4. Hone your basic skills needed for research

Focus on your Coursework

Almost all the PhD programs have an element of coursework. The number of courses and credits might differ from country to country and between institutions. There are many professors who think coursework is a barrier to do research and advise to spend little time on coursework. In my opinion, give importance to coursework. There are many reasons why I think so:

1. Many scholarship criteria will include a minimal CAP (Cumulative Average Point) or GPA (Grade Point Average) or CGPA (Cumulative Grade Point Average). Most commonly, it would be 3.0 or 3.5 out of 4.0! You

might do well in research in the first year and even have a published paper but if you don't satisfy the minimal CAP requirement, your scholarship might not be renewed. While the supervisors might play a role in justifying your continued scholarship by evidence of your research potential, it is wise enough to satisfy the minimal requirement. That would be the simplest and easiest thing to do than complicate your case and be uncertain about the outcome.

2. If you choose the courses carefully, the coursework can directly help your PhD research. For example, if your project involves Finite Element Analysis (FEA), choosing a graduate level / advanced level FEA course will help hone your skills. Most of the advanced level courses will contain a project component (individual or group). If it is permitted by the course instructor, you could choose a project that is related to your research! In other cases, you could learn the theory behind your research by learning the basic science as part of the courses. Your group might be working more on applied research but the courses you choose or take might help you dive deeper into the science behind it, thereby augmenting your base to come up with an even better idea for the applied research.

3. Your supervisor might offer a course which could be very useful to get to know him/her better. The course will not only teach you the basics of your research area as your supervisor is teaching it (mostly Professors teach graduate courses in their area of expertise) but will also help you understand your professor's personality and thinking pattern.

4. Coursework is when you will get to know and be with the other graduate students. This is important as a PhD

student as this network might and in most cases will be your support mechanism. When you have some frustrations with your supervisor or the group members and if you cannot discuss these things within your group, the friends and peers that you got to know and have a relationship with, in other groups, will go a long way in helping you. Not only that but also help you expand your knowledge into other areas of research. You will have chances to discuss your research with them and get to hear about their work, resulting in knowledge enrichment and possible collaboration in the future.

Choose your courses wisely! Like I said in one of the points above, choose courses that would help your research. Make a list of preferred courses and discuss with your supervisor. Your supervisor(s) might already have a list of courses that they think would be important for you to take.

Do a thorough literature review

As you sail through your courses, the next important thing that should be done in parallel is a thorough literature review of your field. Get to know the field that you are going to work on for the next 4 to 6 years. How was the field of research in the beginning? How far has it grown? What is the current research happening in the field? What are the different directions within the field that researchers work on? What are the main challenges that need to be addressed in the field? Get answers to these questions by reading a lot of research papers. I recommend reading at least 5-10 papers per week. Strive to read one paper a day!

Take notes! You might struggle at the beginning with jargon or other technicalities in the field but as you read more and more, you will become more comfortable.

Talk with your peers in the lab, post-docs and senior PhD students to learn more about the field. Learn about various projects happening in the lab. Many groups have regular weekly or bi-weekly lab meetings, which would be a great source of knowledge. If your group doesn't have one, then talk informally to the group members. Attend conferences and talks happening in your university. Attend seminars that are organized by your department. I bet you that you will find these seminars interesting and will open your mind to greater possibilities! Sadly, many students think attending seminars is a waste of time. I agree that some seminars might be boring and not of any use, but do not generalize. Many graduate schools had made it mandatory to attend a number of seminars and write a 1- or 2-page report as part of the PhD requirements.

Identify the gaps – novelty stems out of it!

The main purpose of doing a thorough literature review is not just to understand the field but to critically understand the gaps or challenges! If you just read a lot of papers without identifying the connections between them, the challenges that they have addressed and what remains to be addressed, you are not doing due diligence to your literature review. How true it is to say, "If you can't measure it, you can't improve it". In other words, if you don't know the baseline, you can't set a target. It is a must to know not only the advancements in your field of research but also the gaps that require attention.

When you start reading the papers, for a few weeks or months, you will be in the 'knowledge gleaning phase'. You will read to understand the field, the techniques used in the field, etc. And don't stop with that phase! The next phase is the 'critique phase' where you need to analyze the methods / works critically to see what's been done right, what's wrong, and what's not addressed.

Finding the gaps or challenges in your field is very critical and I cannot emphasize it enough! The novelty of your approach will stem out of the identified gaps / challenges. 'Necessity is the mother of invention' but identifying the necessities is the necessary first step! While some of the students start on a predefined project (as part of a project grant / funding), there might be some preliminary literature review done by the grant writing team including your professor. It is a good starting point but dive deep!

Hone your basic skills needed for research

Another important first step as you start your PhD is to learn or hone the basic skills needed for your research. If you are planning to work on computational projects, learn and become a master of the required software. If you plan doing applied research, learn the experimental techniques. Again, I cannot emphasize enough of this point. Some skills might take half a year to one year, make sure you devote that time in the first year of your PhD. Given the increasing inter-disciplinary nature of the projects, you might have to step out of your comfort zone into unexplored territories. For example, I was a Mechanical Engineering major and I started my PhD in Mechanical Engineering but my PhD topic was bioprinting which necessitated cell culture training. Proper cell culture training and practice might take up to 6 months to learn! Identify the skills required for your research at the beginning and start learning or honing the required skills accordingly!

These four basic things would give you a good start. Remember, "Well begun is half done!".

> "*The main purpose of doing a thorough literature review is not just to understand the field but to critically understand the gaps or challenges! If you just read a lot of papers without identifying the connections between them, the challenges that they have addressed and what remains to be addressed, you are not doing due diligence to your literature review.*
>
> *-Vijayavenkataraman Sanjairaj*"

> "*Finding the gaps or challenges in your field is very critical and I cannot emphasize it enough! The novelty of your approach will stem out of the identified gaps / challenges. 'Necessity is the mother of invention' but identifying the necessities is the necessary first step!*
>
> *-Vijayavenkataraman Sanjairaj*"

CHAPTER X

Planning to fail failing!

Many times, failure is not due to unexpected happenings but due to lack of adequate planning. During my weekly group meetings, I keep telling my staff and students, "80% Planning and 20% Execution"! I think they would have gotten tired of hearing it, but I am not! If you fail to plan, you plan to fail! Embarking on a PhD is such a huge commitment that planning becomes even more critical.

I will give a few tips on how to plan your PhD journey:

Start with a big picture!

Always start with a big picture! That's the best plan to fail failing! When you start your PhD, like I have written in the previous chapter, you will do a thorough literature review to identify the gaps / challenges in the field. Start from that point and draw a big picture around it. I will give an example.

> *"Many times, failure is not due to unexpected happenings but due to lack of adequate planning. During my weekly group meetings, I keep telling my staff and students, "80% Planning and 20% Execution"! I think they would have gotten tired of hearing it, but I am not! If you fail to plan, you plan to fail!*
>
> *-Vijayavenkataraman Sanjairaj"*

Your topic is 3D Printing and you have done a thorough literature review. The gaps that you found are affordability and long printing time. Let us take, for example, you want to reduce the printing time by speeding up the process. You could think of speeding up the process in different ways, using multi-nozzles / printheads / lasers, increasing the speed of the existing movable systems without compromising the quality of printing, or coming up with a completely new technique (volume printing) that would save time! Evaluate each of these approaches and see which is worth pursuing! The second area would be on the materials. Optimize and print using your improved technique or new technique with a variety of materials. Third comes the applications, it could be aerospace or biomedical applications. As you can see, we started from the identified gaps and we painted a big picture around it!

I gave an engineering example. Your area of research might be very different but the approach remains the same. Painting a big picture with a starting point (which is the gap or challenge you identified through literature review). You might struggle at the beginning at each step! Don't lose heart! This is where your peers, colleagues, post-docs and most importantly your Professor / Supervisor comes into play! When you do your part, they would be happy to jump in and guide you. I have observed time and again that some students expect the Professor to readily give a problem to work on. While this is justified for a capstone or final year project at undergraduate level, I personally feel the approach is not justified for PhD level study. If the PhD students are not trained to critically review the literature, identify the gaps, propose solutions, test critically and form conclusions, then the training is incomplete! Even if you embark on a predefined project, follow these steps, else you will be missing important life lessons of your PhD journey!

Set reasonable expectations

The second part of planning comes in setting up your goals for PhD. Some of the Professors define the expectations for you when you start your PhD. The expectations might be in the form of:

1. Number of journal / conference papers
2. Quality of journals / conferences
3. Patents
4. Monographs / books
5. Artworks / installations

> "*I have observed time and again that some students expect the Professor to readily give a problem to work on. While this is justified for a capstone or final year project at undergraduate level, I personally feel the approach is not justified for PhD level study. If the PhD students are not trained to critically review the literature, identify the gaps, propose solutions, test critically and form conclusions, then the training is incomplete!*
>
> *-Vijayavenkataraman Sanjairaj* "

If the Professor sets up these expectations for you, good! If not, set reasonable expectations, after all, it is your PhD! I want to give a word of caution here. Some Professors do not give these expectations and they will seem to you to be the sweetest supervisors in the department. They would even allow you to submit your thesis without any publications or patents. At the end, after all the emotional farewell, when you are in the job market, you will actually feel the pinch! I wouldn't blame the supervisors as each one has their own style of handling / guiding the students. If your supervisor is the sweetest one, then take advantage of that fact in the right way, use that freedom to set your expectations and achieve your goals! Not otherwise!

The key here is to understand your field of research better. Only if you do that, can you set 'reasonable' expectations! Materials Science, for example, can have an expectation of 12 journal papers but that's nearly impossible in Biology! Look out and collect your data. Analyze, benchmark and set your expectations accordingly.

Chart a clear path

You know the big picture and you have your expectations set. The next step is to chart a plan to fulfil those expectations. Say for example, you have set your goal to have 6 publications out of your thesis. You cannot straightaway divide 6 by the number of years of PhD and chart a plan. Remember the learning curve is steep at the beginning, you have coursework to do in the first year and then you have your qualifying exam at the end of first year, etc.

Your first priority would be to complete the coursework satisfactorily to ensure continuity of your scholarship.

Second would be to pass your qualifying exam – standards and format differ from institution to institution and from department to department within the same institution. Check with your department the expectations of the exam, consult with your seniors who have already taken it and be well prepared.

Third is your critical literature review and identification of gaps / challenges – I would highly encourage you to submit a review paper at the end of this exercise in the first year of your PhD as this will be a morale boost for the students. Some Professors might agree and some may not, for many reasons, which I wouldn't talk about here. But, if your supervisor agrees to it, then great!

Fourth is to learn and hone all the skills required to execute your project. This should happen during the first year too! It could be software, or operating a machine or learning a technique.

Fifth is to try and replicate the experiments already done successfully! This could again be a coding, or an experiment; this could be from your own group what your seniors did or could be from a published article. This would ensure that you are all set to go!

Sixth is to come up with a plan for your first research work (a journal paper / conference / any other form)! I will talk about this in detail in the upcoming chapters but plan for research work. Set a timeline for it. It could be right before your qualifying exam, or in the third semester or the following summer or it could be the deadline for a prestigious conference in your field!

Seventh is to come up with a plan for achieving the goal you set. If it is 6 publications, then the first is done in the previous step. Build on it and charter the plan for the other 5. It could be 1 in the second year, 2 in the third year, 2 or 3 in the final year.

All looks fine so far! You might ask "Do you think all I plan is going to happen? In the same way as I planned?" If the answer is yes, then you are one of the luckiest PhD students out there in the world! The answer for the majority would be a big "No!" And that's why I have the next chapter titled "Expect the Unexpected!". Expecting the unexpected is an art and I will teach you some of the tips about it. Some of you might think it is worth planning as there will be unexpected things happening anyway. This is a dangerous thought and a grave mistake if you think so. It is akin to not booking a flight ticket thinking the flight might get cancelled or rescheduled (especially during the COVID times!). The key message is "Plan", if you fail to plan, you plan to fail!

> *"Expecting the unexpected is an art! Some of you might think it is worth planning as there will be unexpected things happening anyway. This is a dangerous thought and a grave mistake if you think so. It is akin to not booking a flight ticket thinking the flight might get cancelled or rescheduled (especially during the COVID times!). The key message is "Plan", if you fail to plan, you plan to fail!*
>
> *-Vijayavenkataraman Sanjairaj"*

CHAPTER XI

Expect the unexpected!

Expecting the unexpected is an art! If only we could internalize the process, we will have a pre-solved answer key to many problems that come our way! Even if you don't have a solution handbook in the process, at the least, you will not panic when the actual problem comes because you have already 'internalized' it! Some may argue that the whole approach of expecting the unexpected is a very pessimistic approach. I cannot help but disagree. It is never pessimistic to expect the unexpected but to stop acting / losing peace / panicking as you expect the unexpected that makes you pessimistic. Expect the unexpected not to trouble your mind but to train your mind! It is good to be positive and be positive, at the same time, prepare for negatives as and when challenges arise, if at all challenges arise! The approach could be summarized in a beautiful sentence, "Hope for the best, prepare for the worst and be unsurprised by anything in between!".

> *"It is never pessimistic to expect the unexpected but to stop acting / losing peace / panicking as you expect the unexpected that makes you pessimistic. Expect the unexpected not to trouble your mind but to train your mind!*
>
> *-Vijayavenkataraman Sanjairaj"*

Now that I have justified the intent behind the approach of expecting the unexpected, let us talk about your PhD. I have mentioned enough times already, throughout the chapters, that a PhD is a long-term commitment and will play a significant role in (re)defining your career. It is natural for challenges to come your way. I will talk about a few challenges that you might face and ways of tackling them. Take these thoughts as possible options to tackle the challenges that come your way and not a verbatim to follow. Challenges are universal but the nature of those challenges are not! Many times, people are the key behind those challenges (ego to be precise) and hence, have to be dealt differently case by case.

Challenges are universal but the nature of those challenges are not! Many times, people are the key behind those challenges (ego to be precise) and hence, have to be dealt differently case by case. - Vijayavenkataraman Sanjairaj

I will categorize the challenges into a few groups to deal with them better:

1. Supervisor-Student challenges
2. Peer challenges
3. Technical challenges
4. Financial challenges
5. Personal challenges

1.Supervisor-Student Challenges

I have told this before in one of the chapters and I repeat again: Your relationship with your PhD supervisor / Professor / guide / mentor is one of the major factors that would determine the success of your PhD! All are human beings and "To err is human!". It is natural that this relationship might turn bitter at some point of time. The first thing to understand is that it is 'natural'! Where there are two human beings, differences ought to be there. That is the beauty of creation and our very existence. Once you accept that this is common, the rest becomes easier. You will be objective rather than being emotional when such a situation arises.

The nature of misunderstandings might be different but I give a template to follow.

1. The second step (first step is accepting the fact that differences are unavoidable) is to introspect yourself.
2. Remove the person (your supervisor as a person) behind the remarks / points / criticisms and just take the remarks / points / criticisms.
3. Introspect to see if those remarks / points / criticisms are valid. Be true to yourself!
4. If it is true, then act on it!
5. If it is not, think of the intent behind the remarks. Is it a misunderstanding? Can you give more facts / data to clarify? If yes, then do it!
6. Do you think it is really unfair and unjustified remarks? Say so! It is your duty to express yourself.
7. If you are unclear, seek clarifications!
8. If you are unable to handle it yourself, talk with people you feel comfortable and trust-worthy, most importantly honest who would give candid feedback. Seek their opinion and see if you are in the wrong.
9. After all these steps, if you still feel and are sure the remarks are unfair, talk to clarify. If the communication is sensible and the parties understand each other, everything is settled and move on.
10. Take steps and make sure the future communications / behaviors prevent the recurrence of the same / similar

incidents.

11. If the clarification / communication (step 9) didn't go well, give it some more time. Time heals.

Even after your best possible efforts, if you still feel you are uncomfortable, feel free and confident to move on – be it to another group / supervisor (if that is possible), start afresh at another institution, or go (back) to the industry! – there is nothing to be ashamed of! This is not a knee-jerk reaction or a foolish decision, you have tried through all the above steps and did your best! Don't lose hope and be confident! Take some time to recover and move on! Many times, the issues really don't escalate to this level. If you can just ignore these issues in a way that it doesn't affect you anymore but you have all the other possible supports, just continue and finish your PhD!

2. Peer Challenges

Relationship issues might come up with the post-docs, technicians, other PhD students or your peers. The first thing to do is to have clarity about the issue, just follow the same steps as in the previous point. Solve it within the team personally as far as possible. If it goes beyond, the good thing here is that you have a supervisor to whom you can escalate things. Assuming the Professor is sensible, the issue would be resolved amicably. Again, take steps and make sure the future communications / behaviours prevent the recurrence of the same / similar incidents. An approach of "agree to disagree but still continue working" might work more easily with the peer challenges than the supervisor-student challenges. If that is the last resort, go for it! Most importantly, don't carry the bitterness in your heart, you will ruin your peace and more relationships!

3. Technical Challenges

PhD is all about exploring new things and solving challenges. Don't panic or be disheartened by failures. While the first two challenges are personality-related, these challenges are all about technicality! It is very well under your control and of course you are there to solve it! If you plan something with an expectation and the end result is something else, don't take it as a 'failure'! You just achieved / got something contrary to your expectations! If Edison hadn't discarded the 9,999 ways that didn't work, the 1 step to the light bulb would not have come forth. I quote, "If I find 10,000 ways something won't work, I haven't failed. I am not discouraged because every wrong attempt discarded is another step forward." JK Rowling's 'Harry Potter and The Philosopher's Stone' was rejected by 12 publishers before it was finally accepted and the rest is history! Walt Disney was denied financial support 302 times before he managed to bring to fruition his idea of "Disneyland"! Ha! Now, I am satisfied with giving enough examples, not only from Engineering or Science but from arts, humanities, and theatre!

4. Financial Challenges

This might be something completely new to you or you haven't thought about it! Yes, there might be financial challenges too! Research depends on funding! And a failure to acquire external funding on time might delay or stall your progress. Do not think it is now impossible to continue your PhD and brood over your efforts! Everything is learning! Nobody can take away the skills that you gained and that is the greatest asset! Re-strategize things! Most of the cases, the Professor would already have a solution. Nothing to worry about! Think of what best you can do within your constraints. Look at other alternate options: collaboration with another institution or industry? DIY if possible? Can you substitute experiment with computational work? This strategy is very much applicable to the technical challenges as well. Being open (an open mind) is the first and most important step.

5.Personal Challenges

There might be a lot of other personal challenges too! Family issues, health issues, personal relationship issues and what not! It is impossible not to be hurt and separate personal and professional things! Both go hand in hand. Taking care of yourself is more important. If you are not well physically, mentally, or emotionally, you will not only spoil yourself but make the whole professional setting messy! In the process, you will hurt other people in your team. Give it some time to heal! It is okay to be honest about the issues and take a break, if it is required. And do not be disheartened that your best efforts in the professional space are getting affected by the personal challenges! You, as a person, are more significant than what you do. In other words, "Who you are is more significant than what you accomplish!"

I can write thousands and thousands of chapters, articles, and books on just overcoming challenges and moving forward, given that each challenge is unique and the solution has to be customized! However, I attempted to just give a drop of the types of challenges and a few ways to tackle them and move on. I am quite sure that these challenges will make you stronger and wiser, more mature and skilled, and mould you into a better you!

"Do not be disheartened that your best efforts in the professional space are getting affected by the personal challenges! You, as a person, are more significant than what you do. In other words, "Who you are is more significant than what you accomplish!"

-Vijayavenkataraman Sanjairaj"

"I am quite sure that challenges will make you stronger and wiser, more mature and skilled, and mould you into a better you!

-Vijayavenkataraman Sanjairaj"

CHAPTER XII

Smartly hard-work and not hardly smart-work!

We have been hearing about the differences between smart work and hard work often through social media. I personally feel the over-emphasis on 'smartness' leads one to think working hard is actually a bad thing and is equivalent to a donkey job. To alleviate such concerns, I titled this chapter as 'smartly hard-work', emphasizing the importance of both smartness and hard-working. When it comes to doing a PhD, although only 2% or less of the whole population goes to do it, there is a notion that all they have to do is hard-work! I want to talk about the importance of smartness in doing a PhD, the thin line between smartness and chicanery, what hard-working means and why combining both to 'smartly hard-work' will greatly impact the quality of your PhD or even your life

The importance of Smartness

There is an implicit bias inherent in all human beings when they hear the words 'hard work' and 'smart work'. People usually associate hard work to slogging with physical activity and smart work has something to do with the brain or mental activity. It might have been partially true until a couple of decades ago when hard-working people were either peasants or blue-collar workers while smart working people were landlords or business owners. I say partially true because even the landlords or business owners have to work hard to keep the business running. They might not actually do the so-called 'real work' by ploughing the field or work in a production line but they have to know and lead 'when to do what' in order for the business to be profitable, out of which the peasants and laborers are paid. Once we understand that almost all of the successful people had actually toiled hard to achieve that success and 'smartness' doesn't necessarily mean some 'shortcuts' or 'tricks' to achieve success, we can move on to see what smartness really means. Everybody would have heard about the story of the woodcutter, not the story of the honest woodcutter and the axe but a more modern woodcutter with a blunt axe.

For those who haven't heard the story, an abridged version: Once upon a time, there was a strong woodcutter. His productivity continuously declined day by day because he didn't sharpen the axe. He was so busy cutting the trees that he thought it wasn't really important to sharpen the axe.

> *"Almost all of the successful people had actually toiled hard to achieve that success and 'smartness' does not necessarily mean some 'shortcuts' or 'tricks' to achieve success!*
>
> *-Vijayavenkataraman Sanjairaj"*

It might seem very obvious, logical, and common sense because we have heard this story before but what we do not realize is we actually do the same thing in our 'work space', be it research or business or life. When was the last time you learnt something new about your work or in your field? How much effort or time have you spent upgrading your perspectives or thinking or skills? Corporates might do these training as part of their strategy but how many employees are really interested in being part of those training and excited about 'learning'? Are we not the same as the woodcutter? Going back to the story of the woodcutter, 'sharpening the axe' is the 'smartness'. Now, will sharpening the axe alone suffice? Of course, not! Unless you work hard on cutting the tree, there will not be any success. At the same time, if the axe is not sharpened, all the hard work that is put in will not yield the results that the hard work really meant to yield or deserve.

> *"Going back to the story of the woodcutter, 'sharpening the axe' is the 'smartness'. Now, will sharpening the axe alone suffice? Of course, not! Unless you work hard on cutting the tree, there will not be any success. At the same time, if the axe is not sharpened, all the hard work that is put in will not yield the results that the hard work really meant to yield or deserve.*
>
> *-Vijayavenkataraman Sanjairaj"*

Apply this to your PhD! Doing experiments is important and that's hard work. You have to toil in the lab, change the experimental setups and parameters, repeat and repeat until you achieve the intended results. But if you are not even aware of the big picture (i.e.) what challenge are you trying to address, what is the big picture and why are you doing these experiments in the first place, what parameters to change and why, you will not go far! If you don't do your literature review properly, you might find, when it is too late, that people have already found a better way or solution that you have been working on for so long! If you are not aware that there is equipment that can simplify the procedure and which your lab can afford to buy, you will be wasting time unnecessarily on things which are not effective and end up being inefficient! Smartness comes into play in all of the above scenarios.

The thin line between smartness and chicanery!

On one hand, there are people who think hard-working is such a stupid thing and menial but on the other hand, there are people who think smart-working means playing tricks, deceiving or cunning! I don't blame them because those thoughts come out of their experience where they are personally deceived by a smart person despite all their hard work. There is a very thin line between smartness and chicanery- make sure you don't cross the border to the worse side! I will give a general example before delving into academic dishonesty. You want to sell your property and you know there is a defect in the property which is not very visible or easily identifiable. You might think you are smart in selling the property without disclosing the defect but indeed you are cheating the other person. You can be sued for half-truths by contract law! You will lose your credibility, end of the story! The same applies to research as well. Some acts might have a clear distinction between right and wrong, for example, fabrication or falsification of data but there are acts which could be justified as 'legally right but ethically wrong'. For example, misleading use of statistical methods or distorted interpretation of the results fall in this grey area. You might legally justify that you were unaware of the bias or the effect of using a particular statistical method but you will be accountable and lose your credibility. You must 'smartly work hard' beforehand to alleviate these mistakes from happening in the first place! There have been many examples from all over the world, be it Professor Robert Slutsky of UC San Diego, USA or Professor Yoshitaka Fujii of Toho University, Japan or Professor Joachim Boldt of the University of Giessen, Germany. All of them would have thought they are smart enough to falsify or misrepresent data but the truth would be known one day or the other!

Quitting your PhD half-way or doing a mediocre PhD is much better than a dishonest star-studded PhD! The 'publish or perish' culture in academia might tempt you to do otherwise but beware! Never compromise your integrity for cheap gains! You might think you are smart but you will be the best among the ludicrous at the end!

> "*Quitting your PhD half-way or doing a mediocre PhD is much better than a dishonest star-studded PhD! The 'publish or perish' culture in academia might tempt you to do otherwise but beware! Never compromise your integrity for cheap gains! You might think you are smart but you will be the best among the ludicrous at the end!*
>
> *-Vijayavenkataraman Sanjairaj*"

Smartly hard-work and not hardly smart-work!

I hope I have given a complete picture of the importance of both hard-work and smart-work. I will not even think twice to say that hard-work and smart-work should be the two sides of a coin! To achieve success, not a dishonest low-value success that comes out of deception, but a well-deserved high-ranked success, smartly hard working is essential. This is where my earlier advice on "80% planning and 20% execution" rule comes into play. Well-begun is half done! Beginning well by planning and putting all your heart and mind in executing the plan will be a (open) secret formula for smartly hard working to achieve success. I want to redefine success here as well. Success always doesn't mean achieving something that the society expects you to achieve but it is a sense of personal accomplishment.

> *"Success always doesn't mean achieving something that the society expects you to achieve but it is a sense of personal accomplishment.*
>
> *-Vijayavenkataraman Sanjairaj"*

Society might expect you to have a paper published in prestigious journals such as Nature or Science, by some hook or crook, at the end of your PhD. If you achieve it honestly, yes, of course, it is a huge success and celebrate! You should not be discouraged if you couldn't get a Nature or Science paper despite all your sincere smart-hard-work! The very satisfaction of having put all your heart and mind into success! While it might be easier to find a job with such publications, you will eventually be successful because you are trustworthy!

CHAPTER XIII

Mid-(PhD)life crisis

Elliott Jaques coined the term 'mid-life crisis' to describe the psychological crisis that middle-aged (45-65 years old typically) people undergo due to various reasons including the feeling of unaccomplishment in life that lead to frustration, depression, anxiety, and other intense negative feelings. Similarly, almost all PhD students face a situation sometime during their PhD journey of extreme negativity that they consider quitting their PhD. It is very rare to see a PhD student who has not experienced such a thing. For some students, it occurs within a year of starting their PhD, for others it might be at the middle of their PhD and for some others, it could be at the very end of their PhD! I will give specific examples of a few scenarios and how to successfully overcome the crisis when it ensues!

1.Analyse the reasons behind the crisis

The first thing that we should do whenever we face a crisis, be it in life, or during the PhD, is to analyze the reasons behind the crisis. Our emotions will always have an upper hand during a crisis and prevent us from thinking logically about it. Give it some time, let your emotions calm down. Take a break! After the break, don't again go into the regular working because you are getting into that vicious cycle of working, breaking down, taking a break, and back to work. Sit and analyze the reasons behind your frustrations. There might be many reasons, I will talk about a few:

- You are not carved out for a PhD! – Like I said in previous chapters, PhD is not something that you cannot afford to lose or cannot live without – Think deeply if the lack of interest or capability is what is causing the crisis
- Chemistry between you and your supervisor or with your team is not good – you might think that you are progressing well but your supervisor thinks otherwise – you feel you plan your experiments well but your team might think otherwise – you go to a meeting with your results thinking you will be appreciated but you're scolded or scoffed at
- You might be really interested in pursuing a PhD and has all the capability but the topic is of no interest to you (contrary to what you thought before choosing the topic)
- You might be really interested in pursuing a PhD and has all the capability and you also like the topic but the group / department / Professor does not have the necessary resources which forces you to underperform
- Many a times, frustrations from your personal life might carry over to your professional life and even a slight disturbance at the workplace might put you off

These are some of the reasons that you might come up with. Think and analyse deeply as to what is the main reason behind the crisis or frustration or your underperformance. Crisis is not caused by a one-time incident but it is an accumulation of incidents over time that is triggered by one incident when it reaches a threshold. It is wise not to just think of that one incident that triggered the crisis but rather the whole series of incidents that brought you to the flash point. Think of all those incidents and see if your reasoning is right. Your solution will be right only if your problem identification is accurate!

2. Think of possible solutions

Once you have identified the problem behind the crisis, the next step is to think of possible solutions. While this may sound very elementary, it is actually a very difficult process. If you are not confident in your problem identification, talk to people and discuss your situation. Make sure they are not gossipers, dogmatic, or drama kings or queens. Talk to people whom you think will assess and give fair and balanced suggestions or opinions. I will talk about the possible solutions for some of the scenarios that we have seen in the previous section:

You are not carved out for a PhD! – The solution is very simple, Quit! – People might tell you are a coward or criticize you for failing but don't bother. It is not wise to jump into the sea without knowing how to swim – your friend might mock at you that you are a coward and afraid of water but if something happens to you after you jump, the same crowd would tell you are foolish to jump into the sea without knowing how to swim. Ignore what others will think or say about you if you quit. If you are confident that PhD is not the cup of tea for you, decide to quit. I know many people personally who quit their PhD but went on to do very well in their career. When I joined my PhD, there was another PhD student in my group who joined in the previous intake. He was a bright student and did very well in his courses and research. One year into his PhD, he realised PhD wasn't for him – he was still interested in the area of his work and though the supervisor is micro-managing and nagging type, he managed without any problems so far – but then he felt and was sure that PhD wasn't for him. He did not take that decision in a day; it was a long-thought decision – he quit and went back to his country and started a firm in the same area of his research and went on to do well.

Group dynamics – Chemistry between you and your supervisor or with your team is not good – you might think that you are progressing well but your supervisor thinks otherwise – you feel you plan your experiments well but your team might think otherwise – you go to a meeting with your results thinking you'll get appreciation but you're scolded or scoffed at – there are various solutions that you have to think through – if you don't gel well with your supervisor, know the reason behind it. Is it due to the knowledge gap? Or working styles? Or any other illogical reason (race, nationality, implicit bias, etc.)? If it is the latter, then express the same to your supervisor, he / she might be doing it without knowing they are doing it or hurting you – if that doesn't solve the issue, look for supervisors whom you think will suit you and if they are ready to take you over as their student. If the problem is with your team members, see if you can solve them by talking over, finding a common ground, or in the worst case by avoiding or ignoring them. If it goes overboard, consult with your supervisor. One thing to remember is wherever you are, at any point of time in your life, you will have such people in your life and you have to deal with them – escapism will not help!

You might be really interested in pursuing a PhD and have all the capability but the topic is of no interest to you (contrary to what you thought before choosing the topic) – this is a common problem. The first thing to do is to read more about the topic to see if there are challenges in the field that you could solve with interest. Even after extensive reading, if you still feel the topic doesn't interest you, talk to your supervisor. Seek his opinion and he might be able to convince you. If you're still not interested, explore the possibility of changing your topic with the same supervisor if that's an option and as a last resort, look for other professors or reapply again to another University.

You might be really interested in pursuing a PhD and have all the capability and you also like the topic but the group / department / Professor does not have the necessary resources which forces you to underperform – I faced this problem during my PhD – the resource was a constraint. We had only one old 3D-printer which has only one functionality and the students had difficulty accessing other advanced bioprinters available in the common facility due to faculty politics. Quitting was not an option for me, so I fought back. I conceived novel ideas that could be achieved with the available resources and also wrote proposals to get extra funding and resources – I wrote grants that resulted in close to S$2 million grants to my group, with which I successfully completed my PhD. See what best you can do with the available resources and if you will be satisfied with your outcome. Think of collaborations and getting external funds for your professor, though it is strenuous and time-taking.

Many times, frustrations from your personal life might carry over to your professional life and even a slight disturbance at the workplace might put you off – Take stock of your personal situation, let things calm down. Seek help, many of your colleagues might be going through the same situation and might have become a pro in handling them well – learn from them as to how to cope up – as far as possible, focus on your work when you are in the lab – the key here is that the research topic should be of immense interest to you that you will nearly forget about any other thing!

3.Decide on-time with no regrets

The most common mistake people make is delay in taking a decision for a long time till the situation is out of control. Patience is a virtue and is good but decisions taken out of time are rather futile. If you are convinced that the decision that you take will give you peace and happiness, do so! Life is full of surprises, don't let regrets spoil the surprises!

> "*The most common mistake people make is delay in taking a decision for a long time till the situation is out of control. Patience is a virtue and is good but decisions taken out of time are rather futile. If you are convinced that the decision that you take will give you peace and happiness, do so! Life is full of surprises, don't let regrets spoil the surprises!*
> -Vijayavenkataraman Sanjairaj"

Don't compare yourself with others and ruin your peace. Your colleague who went on to finish his / her PhD might have become a professor but you are working as a science communicator in a humble office – never regret! What is important is if you are happy doing what you're doing!

Never ever think, 'Oh if only had I finished my PhD, I would have been a professor by now'! – yes, you might have become a professor but then you might not have the peace in your heart as you have now as a science communicator.

Each one has a role to play in this world, a scientist who toils hard in the lab to find a vaccine for Covid and the house-keeping staff who sanitizes the building to keep off the virus, both deserve respect!

> *"Each one has a role to play in this world, a scientist who toils hard in the lab to find a vaccine for Covid and the house-keeping staff who sanitizes the building to keep off the virus, both deserve respect!*
>
> *-Vijayavenkataraman Sanjairaj"*

CHAPTER XIV

End of (dark?) days

Congratulations if you have survived your PhD journey and you are almost there. Many people undergo different emotions when they are almost done with something, a job or project or a PhD. Given the strenuous nature of PhD, many will be exhausted, some unwilling to write the thesis, some will realize they do not have a story to write (cohesiveness), others will realize they have to do a set of experiments to complete the last chapter in the thesis, some would be rushing to publish while others will be waiting for the outcome of their submissions. In whatever state of mind, you are in, relax and strengthen yourself.

I titled this chapter as "End of (dark) days" because many feel so. If you don't, lucky you!! You might think that you are almost done but it might turn out that the last few days or months are more strenuous than the previous 4 or 5 years you spent. It depends on how well you have spent the last 4 or 5 years. If you had read the previous chapters of this book, I would have talked and emphasized enough on having a big picture as you start your PhD. Some might not have that big picture even as they near the end of their PhD. They will feel the pinch when they start to write their thesis.

I will talk a little bit about the different emotions people might have or go through, and how to manage those emotions successfully so as to not prevent you from writing your thesis or preparing for your future career. I will also briefly talk about how to plan your thesis.

Exhaustion – Many might feel exhausted as they near the finish line. This is common. Do take some rest and organize your thoughts and thesis chapters. Look back at what all you have done so far – feel proud about your successes and lessons learnt. Encourage yourself and start writing your dissertation / thesis!

Eleventh-hour work – Some of you might realise you have missed an important piece of the work at the last minute or your supervisor might ask you to do one more piece of work so as to strengthen your dissertation. I know it will be irritating to do such a thing at the last minute. But do not hesitate to work! After all, you have patiently worked for many years now and just consider it as the last leg of the race. Mind, do not stop organizing your thoughts about the thesis or stop writing. Do experiments during the day and write in the evenings. Do not panic! If you panic, you will mess up both the work / experiments and also your thesis writing. Even before you start, plan your work well and expect uncertainties. Have plan Bs!

Writer's block – Some of you might be so interested in working 24/7 but writing is something that you hate. Students working in STEM might feel that writing a paper for publication is much easier as you will have your co-authors to help but the thesis is your child! Some universities permit submission of "stapler or sandwich thesis", which is just a collection of already-published journal / conference articles. If your university permits such a thesis, good for you. But many universities have a specific format to write a thesis and you cannot just compile the papers published and submit. Prepare yourself for writing! You can take two approaches depending on your personality. The first approach is to divide the writing into smaller chunks and set a deadline for each. Write one chunk at a time! When I started writing the first chapter of this book, I was not quite sure that I would actually write a book. I have written more than 20,000 words so far, without realizing it! If this approach works for you, take it! But be sure to plan well in advance so that you can complete the whole thesis on time with enough gap in between each chunk. The second approach is to set a deadline, say one week or one month and finish all in one go! Some prefer it this way as they can just finish and get it done as soon as possible. Either approach is good, the important point is maintaining your quality of writing! Don't rush to finish it just to be returned by your supervisor with red marks throughout.

Fear about the future – It is quite natural that you are looking for jobs as you are writing your thesis. It might take a toll on you as each position requires a customized application, cover letter, CV, etc. **Don't let the fear of the future ruin your performance in the present.** Remember that the thesis that you write will play an important role in your career. Time management is the key here again. If you have done your PhD well, you should already be a master of time management. One way to mitigate this fear is to consult your supervisor to ask if he/ she can support you for a few months in his group as a research assistant until you finish your thesis defence. For any reason, if that is not an option, think of taking a break after your thesis submission, if you have that sophistication. If your financial situation is different, then use the time effectively to apply for jobs and attend interviews. This is where your networking skills will help. If you have attended conferences previously and met a few faculties that you think are your potential future postdoc supervisors, it would be much easier in this period. If you are interested in going to industries, had you done internships or industry-relevant projects, that would be helpful.

> *"Don't let the fear of the future ruin your performance in the present.*
>
> *-Vijayavenkataraman Sanjairaj"*

Carelessness – I have seen a few students who become careless at the end of their PhD journey. Beware! You haven't completed your PhD yet and don't let carelessness take over. If your thesis is returned with major changes, you may have to extend your PhD by 3 to 6 months, many times without additional salary or funding. Remember the story of the Hare and the Tortoise? There is much philosophy and perspectives of the story, which we will not go into, at least for now. The point to be taken is do not be overconfident and careless like the hare, you will lose! Be diligent in your efforts till you are done with everything, there is always time to chill and be careless / carefree.

Do not develop hatred / bitterness / enmity with your supervisor – From my experience, many people get to develop some or the other form of bitterness with their supervisor towards the end of their PhD. This might be due to the fact "familiarity breeds contempt". Avoid arguments and unnecessary wars of words. Of course, you can stand up for your rights and put forth your views. My point is, make sure the dissatisfaction that you have developed over the years does not cloud your mind and spark unnecessary conflicts! "If it be possible, as much as lieth in you, live peaceably with all men".

Planning your thesis

The exact structure and content of the dissertation will vary depending on the field. A generic framework would include:

1. **Executive Summary / Abstract** – you must know what it is! Write in a language that out-of-field experts and laymen can quite understand.
2. **Introduction** – this is where you give the "big picture" – introducing the field or area of work – why is it significant – what are the gaps or challenges that you address. Most commonly, the final paragraph of this chapter would conclude with the introduction of the various chapters of the thesis, with a link or connection between the chapters clearly stated.
3. **Literature review** – I have talked in detail about the literature review previously. This chapter should satisfy three objectives: (i) introduce the field to the reader in detail and what has already been done, (ii) clearly identify the gaps or challenges that are yet to be solved, (iii) set a tone for the novelty of your work – how significant or valuable your contribution is to the field.
4. **Chapters** – there could be 3 to 4 chapters, which forms the heart of the thesis. I will not go into the specifics of how the chapters are written as the content will vary for engineering, science, arts, etc. The important thing is establishing the connection between the chapters. It should be like reading a story. For example, in my thesis, Chapter 1 was Introduction, Chapter 2 was Literature review, Chapter 3 was about the novel technique that I used and setting the experimental parameters, Chapter 4 was to make the material conductive as conductivity is important for neural tissues, Chapter 5 was enhancing the conductivity by using novel biodegradable materials,

Chapter 6 was extensive cell culture studies to prove the superiority of conductive scaffolds compared to non-conductive scaffolds and Chapter 7 was Conclusions.

5. **Conclusion** – Summarize the whole thesis – best if it could be bullet points. The chapter will usually include a section on future directions / potential for further works / applications.

6. **References and appendices** – References or bibliography is an important part of the thesis. Make sure you adhere to the same reference style as required by your department or University. Use a reference management software such as Endnote or Mendeley. You might also have appendices.

The length also varies with your field and the University – it may be anywhere between 30,000 to 80,000 words.

Make sure you discuss with your supervisor(s) before you start writing the thesis. Get their inputs and set clear expectations. If you have two supervisors, then strike a common ground. Each of your supervisors may have different and sometimes conflicting expectations. Meeting both of them together, it might make things easier!

Depending on your supervisor's preference, he / she might ask you to send each chapter as and when you finish to give their comments. Some might prefer having the whole draft at once. Clarify the same with your supervisors, so things go smoothly.

Thesis Review Outcome

Your thesis will be sent to a number of internal and external examiners. They might take anywhere between 4 to 12 weeks to examine your thesis and give you their written comments. You will be given sometime to address those comments satisfactorily before your defence date is set. Make sure you carefully address all the comments as they will serve as the main discussion points or questions during the defence.

There are three most common thesis defence outcomes that you can expect:

1. Pass – You are now Dr. X! Congratulations!
2. Minor revisions – as the name suggests, minor corrections or tweaks may be required – the timeline to complete may range from a few days up to 3 months
3. Major revisions – you may have to repeat certain experiments or rewrite part of the thesis – the timeline for revision may range from 3 to 6 months.

Minor revisions, usually, are most common and quite easy to revise. Major revisions might take more time than your plan. The key here is to clearly understand the expectations of the examiner during and / or after the defence before planning your work – be it redoing or rewriting.

CHAPTER XV

PhinisheD – Now What? Academia or Industry?

Congratulations on successfully submitting your thesis! You are almost there! Within a few days or weeks, you will receive your degree completion certificate! Congratulations Dr! You can give yourself a pat on your shoulders for this achievement. Believe me, it's quite an achievement! While some students have the sophistication of taking a break for a few months, some will be busy looking out for the next career move. While I have seen some students being clear about their future, at least in the broadest sense, to continue in academia or go for industries, many are not. Many of the students want to first complete their PhD before thinking about anything else. If you are one of those, then this chapter is for you.

The first option for any PhD graduate is to continue as a postdoc with the same supervisor (if everything goes well and there is funding) as you finish up writing your journal papers and wrap up non-PhD research works that you worked on. It will be a much easier option as you are already used to working in the same environment. It will give you some time to relax and prepare for your next move. Most Professors, if they have funding, will be most happy to support you. If there is lack of funding or for other reasons you are not able to work with the same Professor, look for positions in your collaborator's lab or other Professors within the department or School. The position might be for a year but it will prevent you from stressing out on moving to a different state or country, right after your graduation. If you have already secured a position in another lab or industry elsewhere, absolutely fine! Congratulations! You will be excited enough to move and that excitement will give you the necessary energy to pack, move, and migrate!

Take some time to read about both academia and industry. Academia might seem a natural fit but it isn't always everyone's cup of tea. If you have an open mind, explore both the options. You would, by now, know what it takes to be a professor. You know how postdocs in your group work and you would have already known how your professor works and his responsibilities. The catch here is to explore the opportunities in the industry. Many PhDs think they are not suitable for industries and they are over-qualified. This is only partially true as the gap between academia and PhD is slowly inching to closure.

The best way to know more about opportunities for PhDs in the industry is to contact your University Career Centre first. From my experience, graduate students (especially PhDs) seek less help from the Career Counsellors than undergraduate students. This might be due to the opinion that such centers are exclusively run for less-experienced undergraduate students. This cannot be right. Many Universities have exclusive teams in their career centers to help graduate students and PhDs. Secondly, talk with your seniors who are already placed in good companies. Learn more about their scope of work and responsibilities. Third, try interning in a company of your choice for a few months, even if it is not a paid position (if you can afford). You will get a feel of working in a corporate setting. This experience will be more valuable especially for those who remained in university continuously – Bachelors, Masters and then a PhD – without any industrial experience. Some may be too used to the academic environment and they dislike the corporate setup, while others like the new environment much more than an academic setting. You will not know unless you experience it.

There are many R&D jobs in industries, where a person with a PhD will be seen as an asset. Mind that the R&D department is not exclusively for the PhD holders, there will be bachelors' and masters' graduates working as well. People with PhDs have the option to lead a team of researchers.

Government agencies can be one of the options that you can consider. Highly-qualified people will have more chances of getting into policy-making bodies or governing / advising bodies in the government. For example, many policy-making bodies in the US are headed by people with PhDs. You can also try getting into institutions like National Institute of Health (NIH), National Science Foundation (NSF), Defense Advanced Research Project Agency (DARPA) in the US. There are similar institutions in Europe and other countries, where you stand a high chance of getting in. There might be resident status or citizenship requirements depending on the country, institution or position.

Start-ups are great places to work as well. If you can't start one, join one! Start-ups will definitely give you enough challenges to solve, given your increased appetite after PhD. Many of my friends who did PhD with me, who decided academia is not for them, went on to join start-ups. Beware that Start-up companies provide a challenging environment, with multiple things to learn and execute. The learning curve would be steep and the journey would be exciting, if you love such challenging environments. You will develop leadership skills and a myriad of other non-technical skills.

There are several University administrative positions that would suit PhD holders who are not interested in research or teaching but remain in academia. Offices such as the office of research – supporting the faculties in grant writing and submission, entrepreneurship and incubation centers, career guidance centers, and office of industry liaison – managing the IP, patents, licensing and other university-industry collaboration.

Positions in trusts, foundations, and other non-governmental agencies that fund various forms of research programs are also potential places where you can apply and work.

As you can see, the opportunities are myriad. It is up to you to seek and find which opportunities would suit you and which type of job or organization you will be happy working for.

CHAPTER XVI

Gloria Academia

Academia has been the first choice for those who pursue PhDs for a long time. With the increase in the number of PhD holders and limited positions in the Universities, the trend is changing. More and more industrial positions and entrepreneurial activities are taken up. However, there is still a considerable population of PhDs excited about getting into academia, after all academia hasn't lost its lustre still!

There is a notion that academia means a faculty position only or the ones ultimately leading to a faculty position. This is not true. In my opinion, academia encompasses all positions including post-docs, senior postdocs, researchers, scientists, senior research scientists, and research assistants. Not all PhDs are suitable nor interested to become a faculty. Projecting faculty positions as the 'do or die' in academia is not healthy.

I personally know many experienced researchers with a PhD who remain as research scientists and enjoy doing pure research without being distracted by teaching and other administrative duties. I do not consider them as less valuable compared to faculties like myself, they are an integral part of the research mechanism. I will talk about a few career options in academia in detail in this chapter, outlining the pros and cons. I will also talk about preparing for the faculty position and what it takes to be a faculty.

Research Fellow / Scientist Positions (short-term): It is very rare nowadays to get a faculty position without significant post-doctoral experience. While 3 to 5 years is a norm before you can apply for faculty positions, you can try earlier or later, depending on how confident you are in establishing and leading a lab. There is a giant leap between being a PhD student and becoming a faculty. The post-doc position is a bridge connecting them. How long or how high the bridge should be, depends on your skill-gap. There are certain skills and qualities that you must develop during your postdoc stint, if you aspire to be a faculty.

1. **Independent research:** You must develop your skills and abilities to do independent research. In other words, carve out a niche for yourself. This could be a subset of your PhD topic or your PhD supervisor's research area but not a complete overlap. Or the niche could be more applied research if your PhD was basic research and delving into the basic science if your PhD was applied research. I will give a few examples (apologies, again it is from Engineering). If your PhD was on traditional materials used in solar cells, you could explore the space of organic solar cells or quantum dots. You could also go basic into the underlying concepts, exploring the drifting electrons, electric fields, and the energy conversion process. Choose a professor who would allow executing your individual ideas during your postdoc position. Depending on whether the position is offered as part of a specific grant for a specific project or a more generic funding from the University, the role of post-doctoral researchers varies. If you choose a position which is funded for a specific project, make sure the project completely aligns with your area of interest. Find places where you can go a little extra-mile to explore certain phenomena that you are interested in, beyond the scope of the project.

2. **Teaching experience:** Most postdoc positions will not offer any teaching experience per se. Explore opportunities with your professor to take guest lectures, prepare class notes or leading tutorials. Any type of teaching experience is good.

3. **People-management skills:** One of the most-important skills to succeed as a faculty is people-management skills. If you are an introvert, nothing wrong, but learn how to manage people effectively with your personality. If you do not know how to work and manage people, most of your time as a faculty will go into relationship problems in the lab. As a postdoc, you will be guiding PhD students and undergraduate researchers. Learn and hone your people-management skills. Have a keen eye and mind to understand which strategies work and which don't, the categories of people you work with and their personalities, and the best way to work with them.

4. **Lab management skills:** While people-management is part of lab management, lab management means much more. You must plan the budget, operating costs, maintaining inventories, maintenance of equipment, hiring people and ensuring their performance and development, and more than all, ensuring sufficient availability of funds. I do not mean to scare you but the faculty position is a mini-CEO position, with end-to-end responsibilities of HR, maintenance, finance, research, publication, teaching and mentoring.

5. **Grant-writing skills:** You must develop skills on writing grants to attract external funding. A single most important skill that would help sustain your lab. Do not hesitate, even for a second, if you get an opportunity to write grants along with your professor.

Tenure-track vs permanent faculty positions: Depending on the country you are applying to; the faculty positions may be broadly classified into two – tenure-track and permanent positions. Tenure-track positions are the most common in the US – the positions are typically 6-year contracts, with a mid-tenure review after 3 years. In the sixth year, you would be expected to submit a tenure docket, which undergoes extensive review. If you succeed, you will be offered a "tenured" position, which is a permanent position. If your tenure application is unsuccessful, you will be given an additional year to look for new opportunities elsewhere. In countries such as UK, the faculty positions are permanent positions (there might be some exceptions such as contract faculties). You are typically inducted as a Lecturer, your promotion to senior lecturer, reader, and Professor positions depends on your performance and experience. In Europe, there are "Group Leader" positions, which might have a teaching component, but are mostly time-bound, say 5 or 6 years – after which you apply for fresh funding or a faculty position.

Research Fellow / Scientist Positions (long-term): A typical academic career track includes 3-5 years of postdoctoral experience, followed by a faculty position. But not all are suitable or interested in faculty positions. They choose to be in long-term research fellow or scientist positions. There is nothing less-prestigious in being a scientist compared to a faculty. Depending on the university or research institution, the career path includes promotion to senior positions such as senior research scientist / fellow and group leader. Institutes such as A*STAR in Singapore have well-drawn career path for non-teaching researchers. The advantage of such positions is that you will be able to continue your research without any teaching responsibilities, if you are not passionate about teaching. The disadvantage is that many research scientist positions are time-bound, subject to availability of funds. For those who want to explore the world, moving to different countries and universities, this is fine. But it comes with a risk and stress associated with finding positions once every few years. For those looking for more permanent positions, look for institutions where you have a long-term career path that is not constrained by funding availability.

Lab Manager: Many Professors and groups look for lab managers, who are experienced in managing research labs, more applicable to PhDs in STEM disciplines. Many postdocs have shifted their career path to become lab managers and they are happy with the position. You get to do research, manage the lab and students, without the pressure that a tenure-track faculty has to take.

Safety / EHS Officers: This is again more applicable to PhDs in STEM disciplines. I personally know someone with a PhD in Biochemistry from US, did 4 years of postdoc in a research institute and then became a EHS safety manager. He takes care of all the Environment, Health, and Safety (EHS) requirements of the labs within the university.

Research administration: Every University has an office of research with various functions. The office not only supports the undergraduate and graduate research but also faculties in the writing, submission, and management of grants.

Entrepreneurship, Innovation and Industry Liaison: If you are passionate about entrepreneurship and innovation, you can either start-up or join the entrepreneurship and innovation cell in the universities, which are increasingly gaining traction. Industry Liaison offices may also be a good choice, dealing with intellectual property rights, patenting, licensing, and other industry-university collaborations.

99

CHAPTER XVII

PhD holders in Industry?

There are plenty of scope and opportunity in the industry for those who have completed their tertiary degrees such as PhD. The key here is to develop "transferable skills". The skills that you learn in academia that could be very useful in industries. For example, if your PhD involves extensive use of software such as Computational Fluid Dynamics (CFD), it is one of the most sought-after skills required in various industries. Some might wonder that their PhDs are in mathematics or philosophy or psychology – what about them? The good thing is, if you have done any kind of PhD, you already have a set of "transferable skills" that you developed, knowingly or unknowingly (or rather consciously or otherwise). If you are not aware of them, know them now.

Transferable Skills:

Communication: Have you done your weekly or biweekly update presentation to your professor? The myriad times that you presented your results and discussed with your peers in team meetings? How about all those conference presentations? Graduate seminars? Oh, the written reports, journal papers, conference proceedings, white papers, grant proposals? Yes, believe it or not, you have done a lot of exercise during your PhD to develop your communication skills – both oral and written. It is, indeed, an asset to any organization!

Critical thinking: I cannot emphasize enough of this skill in the industry. Having completed your PhD, you are trained to think critically. You do not just make split-second decisions emotionally (well, you may still, when it comes to personal stuff!) when it comes to work. You analyze the facts and make logical decisions.

Problem identification, analysis & solving: Remember all those days of slogging with the literature review? What did you exactly do? How many times have your experimental set-ups given you problems? Your coding did not work? How many times did you retry that painting? How long did it take for you to get that emotion right in theatrical practice? What you exactly did and was trained to do was to identify the problem correctly, analyse it and find solutions.

Data Management: You have handled such huge data sets, experimental results, simulations, thousands of lines of codes. Industry values data management and data-driven processes.

Multi-tasking and time management: Course work, research, weekly presentations, teaching assistantships, team meetings, one-on-one meetings with Professors – you have really learnt how to multitask and manage your time effectively and efficiently.

Project and People management, Leadership Skills: You would have executed multiple projects within the duration of your PhD. And without any PMP certification, you have done it well! You would have coordinated your experiments with other people, given tasks to masters' and bachelors' students, navigated your way with the technicians and lab staff – trust me, if you compare your people management / leadership skills before and after your PhD, you will be surprised to realize how much you have grown!

Do you still think, with all these skills you possess, it is that difficult to get you a job in any relevant industry? You will be overqualified for most of the jobs as I had explained in the previous chapters. You have to find the right industry and right job that suits well with your PhD. I have listed a few obvious choices here; it is up to you to explore to the fullest extent possible.

Research Institutes: Research institutes will be a middle-ground between academia and industry. Your working environment will more or less remain the same as your lab or university but you will see corporate governance in place. You can be a scientist, technician, or a Principal Investigator leading a group of researchers in a research institute. You will not lose connection with academia.

R&D Divisions of Companies: Almost all major companies have their R&D divisions. PhDs are most welcome in those divisions. It is not a surprise that Facebook and Amazon hire PhDs for their research wings, be it on Artificial Intelligence or driverless vehicles.

Start-ups: There are so many start-ups out there that require experts like you, who are passionate about translating the technology from bench to the bedside, from labs to the market. While your technical and transferable skills are most valued in a start-up, you can learn much more on the non-technical side such as product strategy, product-market fit, business strategy, marketing, sales, and the whole B2B / B2C process.

Government agencies: Government agencies can be one of the options that you can consider. Highly-qualified people will have more chances of getting into policy-making bodies or governing / advising bodies in the government. For example, many policy-making bodies in the US are headed by people with PhDs. You can also try getting into institutions like National Institute of Health (NIH), National Science Foundation (NSF), Defense Advanced Research Project Agency (DARPA) in the US. There are similar institutions in Europe and other countries, where you stand a high chance of getting in.

Like I said, these are some of the most obvious choices. There is much more to explore, if you have the will and grit to do so! All the best!

CHAPTER XVIII

My PhD journey

I was born in a typical South Indian middle-class family to not so well-educated but loving parents. I did well in my school and was a topper throughout. You might be aware that the competition for seats in top universities in India is absolutely brutal! You can get into prestigious institutions only if you have >99% marks and I know cases where students with even 99% marks could not get into the institutions / courses of their choice. Without digressing much, my cut-off marks for admission were 198.75 out of 200 – more than enough to enter one of the most prestigious and oldest technical institutions in India, the "College of Engineering, Guindy". Mechanical Engineering was the only course that I wanted and I got what I wanted. I did well in my undergraduate studies and managed to get an international summer research scholarship called "Working Internships in Science and Engineering (WISE) Scholarship" from DAAD to intern at Technical University of Munich, Germany. During the senior year of my B.Eng., I was offered a job at Caterpillar India Pvt Ltd (a subsidiary of Caterpillar Inc. in India) as part of campus placements. I worked with Caterpillar for 3 years as a Strategic Sourcing Engineer (aka Buyer), learning the whole B2B process of sourcing. My passion was to become a professor right from the beginning. I wanted to get into an industry before I go for graduate studies because the professors in my university, who had 3+ years of industrial experience before coming to academia, stood out compared to the ones who were in academia throughout. After working at

Caterpillar for exactly 3 years, I thought it was the right time to pursue graduate education. I formally applied to only one university and one department, PhD in Mechanical Engineering at National University of Singapore (NUS). I chose Singapore because it is closer to home, 4 hours by flight from my hometown. And after the initial screening and interview, I got the admission.

I wasn't in touch with academia for three years. The last thing I did was my final year project (or capstone) 3 years ago. So, I joined NUS 6 months before my PhD commenced, as a research assistant to hone my research skills and get used to the academic / research environment again. And thank God, I decided so! The 6 months taught me a lot of life lessons and about the different personalities of the Professors. Girdle up to read everything that I underwent in those tiring 6 months!

The Professor was well-trained in US institutions, was young, in his late 30s and was a tenure-track Assistant Professor. The first 2 weeks went without much trouble. A lot of paperwork, visa formalities, orientation, completion of mandatory EHS courses, setting up bank accounts, HR processes and getting access to the lab. From the third week, I started my preliminary experiments and was continuing to review the literature. There was one other research assistant, one master's student, and one PhD student in the team. The lab was just set up over the last year. The pressure started building up from the second month. I was expected to come up with enough results to write a paper in the next couple of months. I had minimal guidance. The area of research was completely new to me. I did my best to read as many articles as possible and had taken notes filling up a whole notebook. I did my best to understand the subject before delving into the project. But ironically, the Professor was interested only in the output and did not care about 'understanding'. He kept saying, 'just repeat what is in this paper that I published during my postdoc'. That was not as easy as it sounds. Without any proper equipment in the lab and no senior researchers to guide, it was not easy.

Every weekly meeting was tough for us. It was very difficult to explain my thoughts to him because everything would be over-simplified. Any experiment can be done in a couple of days, and any software can be learnt over the weekend. I will give one example. We would be asked to do an experiment. If we tried and it didn't work, we would naturally report it. The response would be to try to make it work and only report that it worked. That was fine – we could try hard to make it work! But the next time you try something and say you tried x y z; you will be scolded for doing things which were not told. Maybe it was a communication problem. I would still want to give the benefit of doubt. Luckily, I didn't have any coursework to do as I haven't started my PhD because coursework is again nothing to him – research and output is very important. Do I have to say the only one PhD student in the lab went through a tough time and he quit at the end of his first year!!

I was very determined to pursue my PhD at any cost and I tried my best to sustain but in vain. I was mentoring one of the undergraduate students for her Final Year Project (or capstone). She went through hell and had suicidal thoughts. She had to seek psychological counselling for depression. She went ahead and complained to the department of how she was treated after she completed her project successfully to her satisfaction (but not to the satisfaction of the Professor though). Again, completely relatable – most students do not finish their PhD/project to their supervisor's satisfaction – I understand – for many reasons.

I lost it as well. I went to meet him personally and told him that I am not in a position to continue PhD with him and sought his permission to do my PhD under another supervisor. He did not agree. Technically, this was possible and was allowed by the University. The PhD scholarship comes from the government / university and not from the Professor's funds. And there were precedents before in the department. Yet, he did not agree. He said there were only two options, either to continue with him or quit my PhD and go back to my country. He even threatened openly that he would write all sorts of negative things about me, if I tried talking to the department or other professors. And he did! I will come to it in a while. I was going through a lot mentally and emotionally. Each faculty has his or her own style of handling the lab and the students. That's perfectly fine. Whatever happened so far was still fine to me, be it the micro-management or being capricious or being overly demanding or humiliating the students, I would still want to give the benefit of doubt to the faculty. Because only God knows how much a tenure-track faculty go through – the stress of establishing himself/herself in a new institution. But treating a student this way and threatening the future of the student? I am not sure! I will let you decide.

I had to start my PhD with him and I did. I was still going through the same hell and I am 3 months into my PhD now. I don't want to write about all the terrible things I underwent. Remember the complaint raised against him by the undergraduate student? That has come to our rescue now! The complaint has reached the department Chair and all of us in the team were called for inquiry. All of us had the same thing to say! And did I say I was also racially targeted? He once told me that Indians have 'fat fingers' and are not suitable to do 'microfluidics'! Really? I don't know if it was just a random joke or he felt funny but it was not funny to us! Finally, I saw light at the end of the tunnel. I had decided to quit my PhD by now, if I were to continue with him. The department now allowed me to choose another supervisor. I was relieved and two supervisors agreed to take me as their PhD student. As customary, the potential supervisor had written to the previous supervisor asking for his opinion. You know what was done? He wrote a nasty email with a lot of unimportant and trivial things, recommending he not take me. His only goal now is to destroy me! I am completely fine if honest things about me was written – I took time to readjust to the research environment or the field is completely new to me so it took time to get the first set of results – whatever be it. But writing unfounded imaginary things with the sole aim of destroying the student's future, I can't imagine! God never let me down! The potential supervisor ignored his email and decided to take me in. And he never regretted his decision! He wrote in my recommendation letter that 'I was the best PhD student among the 50+ students that he had mentored over the last 30 years'!

That was quite long, wasn't it? I even hate to recall those things that would rekindle the negative emotions in me. I have no bitterness towards him and I have completely forgiven. I only pity him. He might have been under the tenure pressure or he was just learning as a young Assistant Professor on handling a team. It might take years to understand human psychology, he might be completely different person now and I wish him well. I thought I must write those things as any student might undergo similar situations in their life. Let it be an inspiration! Before I move on to talk about my real PhD journey briefly, I wanted to tell an interesting incident. After I completed my PhD (my defence was pending), I started applying for faculty positions. I was invited as one of the shortlisted candidates to a very good state university in the US for an in-person interview. I went and did well. I was not offered the position because I haven't defended my thesis yet. You know the surprise? The Professor whom I talked about all this time was also shortlisted for the same position and came to interview before or after me, I learnt later. His tenure application did not go through at NUS and he is now working in the University in the US, where we interviewed together for the same job! Do not be discouraged at any point in your life! Give your best, leave the rest to God!

Now to the actual PhD journey – I have lost close to 6 months into my PhD on the above account. With a new research group and topic, again I had to start from square one on the literature review. My professors now were senior Professors and gave me a free-hand. I enjoyed the freedom and utilized it to the maximum. There was a lack of resources and equipment but I managed well to sail through as I was not micromanaged and the Professors were understanding. I had written several grant proposals back then and got close to S$2 million – a very valuable experience that helps me as a faculty now. My supervisors took me along to the grant proposal interviews to present and answer any queries. I had more than 15 peer-reviewed international journal papers published during my PhD. Was everything so smooth and calm during the process? Of course, not! There were times when I felt lonely, times when I was discouraged with the lack of access to equipment or resources, when collaborators do not actually collaborate, and whatnot. I learnt many valuable life lessons on how to handle people in academia, how to manage the lab, putting myself in the shoes of my postdocs and graduate students, what the department, the university and the wider academic community expects of you and amidst all of these, how to do meaningful research that would benefit the society. I will think of writing down all these in detail in another book, maybe? ☺

CHAPTER XIX

Key takeaways

1. Choosing the right supervisor is the key to completing your PhD not only successfully but in peace!
2. Do not be afraid to face Challenges! Facing challenges is part of the process!
3. Do not be discouraged by unjustified, unfounded, unfair accusations, allegations, or opinions! Give your best in every situation, let your work speak your worth!
4. If you find yourself entangled in a toxic academic environment, seek help, voice your opinion, and do not think twice to quit. Your well-being is much more important than getting a PhD – there are people who need you out there!
5. Refusing the resource and equipment constraint deter you from doing quality work! Do what it takes!
6. Do not compare yourself with others! Each one has their own way of living and excelling in life. Be unique! Find your niche! Aspire high, not in comparison with others! Dream big, work hard and fly high!
7. Be grateful for what you have! Enjoy the present and that's the secret to a hope-filled future!
8. Be humble! You can learn from everyone around you! I remember sharing my thoughts in the farewell dinner that my colleagues in the company gave me when I left – "I learnt from all of you all, both how to be and how not to be!" – sounds philosophical but true! Ever wondered what you can learn from people who are so mean to you?

Learn how not to be mean ☺

9. Be patient! Your time will come. Do not hurry yourself and put your body and mind to mental distress. Do your best and leave the rest – at the appointed time, you will be rewarded!

10. Forgive and forget! Be it an immature supervisor, uncouth students, nagging post-docs, indifferent colleagues – forgive and forget! Maintaining inner peace goes a long way in keeping you hale and healthy and will prevent you from being the same wrong person to your superiors, subordinates, colleagues and students.

All the best for a wonderful start, continuation or completion of your graduate studies! Do write to me your reviews, lessons learnt and most of all, your personal experiences. If this book has helped you in any way, do let me know – not to be proud of but to bask in the happiness of having helped at least a soul!

I hope I earned the privilege of your time! Thank you!

About The Author

Vijay is an Assistant Professor of Mechanical Engineering at New York University Abu Dhabi. He is also affiliated with the Department of Mechanical and Aerospace Engineering at Tandon School of Engineering, New York University, Brooklyn, USA. He is the founder and director of The Vijay Lab at New York University Abu Dhabi, with a focus on 3D printing and Bioprinting for tissue engineering, regenerative medicine, drug testing, and medical devices. He has published over 40 articles in peer-reviewed international journals. He holds editorial positions and serves as editorial board member of several reputed international journals including Artificial Organs (Wiley), International Journal of Bioprinting, Frontiers in Mechanical Engineering, and Micromachines. His works include conductive scaffolds for neural tissue engineering fabricated by electrohydrodynamic jet 3D printing, bioprinting of bi-layer functional human skin constructs, biomimetic scaffolds for tendon and esophageal tissue engineering, architected meta-materials-based design of bone implants for better biomimicry and mitigating the effect of stress-shielding, and development of novel bioinks for bioprinting of soft tissues. He was the recipient of several prestigious awards including the President's Graduate Fellowship for his doctoral studies at the National University of Singapore, Raman Memorial Award, The Sachivothama Sir C.P. Ramasamy Aiyar Scholarship, and WISE (Working Internships in Science and Engineering from DAAD Germany.

How This Book Came To Be

I had many students ask me about the PhD, if it is worth pursuing, how to select a university, what to look for in a research group, career path in academia or industry and surviving the PhD ordeal! Since I had answered hundreds of them already, I thought that is the first topic that I would want to write about. It might seem very obvious to some while others might find it extremely useful but I would pen down in each of the chapters what my thoughts are, from my experience in interacting with a lot of students, ranging from aspiring undergraduate students, both successful and struggling PhD students, and most-importantly the highly ambiguous PhinisheD ones!

The chapters in this book not just focusses on a set of objective things to look for when you decide on your graduate studies. The book is filled with lot of practical things to consider, which I personally felt nobody told me about! Had I known these things before I decided on my graduate studies, I would have been more careful!

www.ingramcontent.com/pod-product-compliance
Lightning Source LLC
Chambersburg PA
CBHW040810120726
48005CB00012B/1369